CHICKEN SOUP
FOR THE INDIAN SOUL

CHICKEN SOUP
FOR THE
INDIAN SOUL

101 Stories to Open the Heart & Rekindle the Spirit

Jack Canfield
Mark Victor Hansen
Raksha Bharadia

westland

We would like to acknowledge the following publishers andindividuals for permission to reprint the following material. (Note: The stories that were penned anonymously, that are in the public domain or that were written by Raksha Bharadia are not included in this listing.)

A Blazer, Red Scarf and Fifty Bucks. Reprinted by permission of Freya Parekh. © 2007 Freya Parekh.

A Cup of Tea. Reprinted by permission of Jagat Sukadia. © 2007 Jagat Sukadia

(Continued on page 297)

westland ltd

Venkat Towers, 165, P.H. Road, Maduravoyal , Chennai 600 095
No. 38/10 (New No.5), Raghava Nagar, New Timber Yard Layout, Bangalore 560 026
Survey No. A - 9, II Floor, Moula Ali Industrial Area, Moula Ali, Hyderabad 500 040
23/181, Anand Nagar, Nehru Road, Santacruz East, Mumbai 400 059
47, Brij Mohan Road, Daryaganj, New Delhi 110 002

Copyright © 2008 Chicken Soup for the Soul Publishing LLC
All rights reserved

First published in India by westland ltd 2008

This edition is published under agreement with Chicken Soup for the Soul Publishing LLC
CSS, Chicken Soup for the Soul and its Logo and Marks are trademarks of
Chicken Soup for the Soul Publishing LLC

10 9 8 7 6 5 4 3

ISBN : 978-81-89975-43-2

This edition is for sale in India, Pakistan, Sri Lanka, Nepal and Bangladesh only

Cover Design: Supriya Saran

Typeset in Palm Springs
by Mindway Design Pvt. Ltd., New Delhi

Printed at Sai Printo Pack Pvt. Ltd. New Delhi

Contents

Introduction

Chicken Soup stories have the power to change lives. I can say this with conviction, for in the course of compiling, editing, and writing for *Chicken Soup for the Indian Soul*, I changed. Allow me to share my experience which, after much deliberation, I realised needs to be related in the Introduction itself.

I have two friends I am extremely close to. Our relationship spans more than a decade. Strangely, serious differences developed with both of them individually within a short span of a month. Not that I had never argued with them before. As with all close ties, we too had had our fair share of conflicts and heated debates. But our bonds of friendship had always held firm, surviving everything. Our estrangements never lasted beyond a few days; in fact, we always came back closer after every estrangement, feeling more for the other, not less.

The argument that I had with them, about a month before I began working on this book, was the worst ever. Close friendship, as much as it comforts and pleases, also makes one vulnerable. We hurt each other in those areas where we knew the other was most sensitive. For the first time in twelve years I found the very foundation of the relationship wobbly. I doubted in all earnestness whether they were my well-wishers at all; they too thought that perhaps the friendship had run its course and it was time to bid adieu. We switched off and more than two months passed.

Then stories for this book began pouring in. I read true stories of people who had lost a love, allowed a relationship to go sour, all over silly ego-issues, misunderstandings that a lack of communication and priorities made appear worse than they were. I also read about people struggling with themselves, of how they overcame unimaginable obstacles, and somehow kept their spirits up despite everything. I read their tributes to loved ones, at times to complete strangers who stepped in and helped them at crucial moments. I read how people kept their focus on the 'whole', while struggling through the unpleasant 'parts'. I read about mistakes which cost one dearly and the feeling of guilt and remorse that never quite left. I read about understanding and self-realisation, about courage and heroism, generosity and kindness—at times from complete strangers—and about forgiveness and its healing power both for the forgiven as well as the one forgiving. Through the stories I saw how people turned their failures into learning opportunities. I witnessed the power of self-belief and following one's convictions with passion and determination. I understood that life truly is what we make of it! Most importantly, I learnt that in the end it is not about how much money one makes, how much fame one achieves, how beautiful or handsome one is—it is about how much love one can give and receive; it is about the kind of relationships one has with oneself and with others; it is about what one sees, the 'part' or the 'whole'... I understood how big life is and how small I had become in my vision of life, of others, even of myself.

One Saturday afternoon, I telephoned my estranged friends and apologised. We made up between sobs ... the stories that

I had been reading were too big for me to hold on to my narrowed sense of them, myself or life!

The 101 stories in this compilation are true stories of people and their life-changing experiences. It encapsulates their learning, defining moments, convictions and understanding. Each story has been told from the heart. If you slow down enough to listen, you will hear not only the written words but the hope, strength, spirit, angst and struggle which the stories carry between their lines. Savour each story as you would a good cup of your favourite brew. Sip the words with leisure. Enjoy the warmth that fills your soul.

Allow yourself to feel the stories. Let your emotions loose. Do they remind you of a person in your life whom you want to thank, ask forgiveness of, something you should have done long ago? Pick up the phone and make the call. Do they want to make you reach out and help someone you had once bypassed? Connect with that person today and do not ignore others who look to you for help and support. Do they make you want to let go of your fears? Then tell yourself, 'I can do it'. Do they make you want to share a story from your life? Pick up a pen and write. These stories are meant to inspire and motivate you.

For some of these stories we went back to the original source and asked them to write or tell it in their own words. We have attributed every story we could to the original source. We have included a contributors' section at the end of the book, where we have listed their names and email ids so that you can contact them yourself if you wish.

I really do hope you enjoy reading this book as much as I have enjoyed compiling it!

1

ON LOVE

When I despair, I remember that all through history the way of truth and love has always won. There have been tyrants and murderers and for a time they seem invincible, but in the end, they always fall ... think of it, always.
        Mohandas Karamchand Gandhi

A Blazer, Red Scarf and Fifty Bucks

I have this college friend, Eric, and one thing that has always intrigued me about him is how he deals with the less privileged.

We have a lot of homeless people that come around our neighbourhood every day, either collecting stuff from our trash or asking for money and food. Walking to and from class, you could come across at least five of them. Most of the time I pass by them, barely noticing their presence because I am so rushed for time, but Eric always takes the second (even if he is in the middle of an important conversation!) to take out his wallet and give the person a dollar.

This may not seem like a big deal, because most students at USC have a dollar to give away. And sure, Eric isn't dead broke, but like all of us film school students, he doesn't have money to squander either. What's more, he doesn't just give them the dollar and walk away—he makes sure he says a good word, sometimes actually sitting down and having a conversation with them. The reason I decided to sit down and write this, though, is because of what happened last night.

Last night, another one of these homeless individuals came up to the house next door. The other four of us there ignore him, but Eric tells him to hold on a second. He goes up to his room, grabs a blazer, a beautiful red scarf his sister gave him for Christmas, and fifty dollars. He runs outside, dresses the man in the blazer, the scarf and then hands the man the money!

I watch from inside the house, and I am brought back to my own life experiences where I understood the capacity for human compassion. As you might imagine, the homeless man was beyond grateful, and he simply said, 'There must be a God.'

Eric walks back in, and I'm totally dumbfounded. I ask him, 'You just said you were broke. Don't you need that money?' 'I have to read something to you,' Eric replies and leads to me to his room where he pulls out this book he's been reading—Gandhi's *Experiments with Truth*. Then, he reads me this quote:

Whenever you are in doubt, or when the self becomes too much with you, apply the following test. Recall the face of the poorest and the weakest man whom you may have seen, and ask yourself if the step you contemplate is going to be of any use to him. Will he gain anything by it? Will it restore him to have control over his own life and destiny? In other words, will it lead to swaraj for the hungry and spiritually starving millions? Then you will find your doubts and yourself melting away.

He shuts the book and says, 'See, it all makes sense.'

I've been thinking about the experience and the quote all day today.

Freya Parekh

A Cup of Tea

I was leaving a dinner party where there was a lot of food left over. I decided to pack some of it and give it to a homeless person on my way back home. At one of the traffic intersections along the way, I saw a handicapped man, Abdul bhai. I took the food over and sat next to him. We started talking and he told me about the brutal accident that had taken both his legs. Soon after, he said, his family disowned him; and society followed suit. Wandering the streets, he had found solace in alcohol.

After he opened his heart to me, I asked him if he wanted to eat. Without hesitation he responded, 'I made some money begging and have eaten enough to fill my stomach. Give this food to somebody else who needs it more.' Abdul bhai was completely inebriated, but he was clear in his response.

During our conversation, he told me he could not remember the last time somebody had spent time with him. Through his stories I learned that, although he begged for money to buy food, he always shared what he collected with others. On the days that he earned too little to feed someone, he would at least buy them tea. And then he offered me a cup.

When we give a little happiness, we get so much more in return. Perhaps Abdul begs on the streets and we assume he has little to give, but that day he filled my heart, and of course the tea was delicious!

Jagat Sukadia

A Miracle Called Commitment

When my wife of thirty-five years, Vimla, suffered her massive brain haemorrhage, I had to help her overcome it. And Vimla was committed to my commitment, for she knew that I would not be able to survive without her.

It was on 13 October 1994 that our lives changed forever. We were vacationing in Laxmangarh, her native place, a small village in Rajasthan. This was an annual ritual: the entire family, including a couple of great-great-grandchildren, united under one roof every year to celebrate the spirit of Navaratri. One evening Vimla began throwing up and then fainted. She regained consciousness with a splitting headache and the local doctor we had called misdiagnosed it as a simple gastric attack. He assured us that she would be fine in a day. For two days she lived from one painkiller to another. On the third morning I knew that something was terribly wrong with my wife. I packed for us ʟoth, drove down to the nearest airport, Jaipur, and took the first flight out to Kolkata.

By the time we landed in Kolkata, Vimla could not even walk down the aircraft steps without assistance. We drove her straight to a hospital in an ambulance. Neurologist Dr Pahari Ghosh took one look at her and diagnosed it as a massive brain haemorrhage. The bleeding had already caused considerable damage.

Vimla was put in ICU and the doctor put her chances of survival to twenty percent. On the third day of hospitalisation, she suffered a paralytic stroke which rendered her entire right side immobile. She lost her speech, her memory and the use of her limbs. For twenty days she hung between life and death. I still remember the doctor's words on the twenty-first day, 'Mr Killa, Vimla is out of danger'. I thanked him profusely as tears rolled down from my eyes. The battle of life had been won, but the battle of living had just begun.

After a month and a half at the hospital Vimla was finally released. We brought her home, bedridden, speech-impaired and with very little memory of her past life. At the age of forty-eight she began her A, B, C's once again with a speech therapist; at eighty-four kilograms she began physiotherapy to relearn how to walk. The entire family pooled in their resources. Grandchildren in the family took charge of her memory. They showed her photographs, spoke of past incidents, sang songs, and slowly but steadily her life came back to her. My son and daughter-in-law shouldered the responsibility of providing food. Friends fixed their schedules to visit her in the afternoons when she was most prone to feeling lonely.

Vimla's days moved with the tick of the clock. There was a time for everything; a schedule that had to be adhered to, by the minute. She went through endless therapies, gulped scores of medicines and had not the speech to express even the pain that she endured. Every minute that I was home we spent in the same room, and when I was at office, I called her every hour. Vimla could not speak much, but to show us all her gratitude, she redoubled her efforts to get well. In three months she showed marked improvement. Soon we were able to go for walks in Victoria Park. The first day we did fifty meters together and I felt as if I had won the biggest trophy ever! Her speech too began coming back. Life inched towards normalcy. Then, in January, we did another MRI as prescribed by the doctor. The scan showed another aneurysm which *had* to be surgically clipped.

On 22 March 1995 Vimla was admitted once again to the Hinduja Hospital, Mumbai. A neurosurgeon performed the complicated, delicate surgery which took seven hours. Though the aneurysm was successfully clipped, Vimla found herself bedridden once again. I still remember the doctor's words, 'A surgery is also an injury; although there is controlled damage, the damage is nevertheless there'. For the second time Vimla lost her memory, whatever speech she had regained and the use of her legs too. Therapy—physio, speech—had to start afresh. Besides, she developed the complication of convulsions as well. The doctor softly warned me to prepare for her gradual decline into depression and to keep her as occupied as possible to delay the same. The word he used was not 'avoid', but 'delay'. He said that such people usually lose their will to live because of loneliness and frustration, and gave Vimla about three years!

I promised myself that I would prove the doctor wrong. Therapies began once again, but this time the progress was painfully slow—just as the doctor had warned. It took Vimla five months to get back on her feet this time. Speech now eluded her completely. Even to communicate that she wanted pickle to spice up her meal was a task both for her and the other who struggled to understand. And most importantly we all had to remember never to lose our cool with her! Again, her days were timed to the minute. Between her morning walks and evenings at the club, her days were filled with therapy and some television. We made sure she was neither lonely nor frustrated.

In 1998 she developed severe backache, it was Bone TB this time. Vimla was bedridden once again. The doctor recommended a nine-month stay in bed. For the first three months she was not allowed to even change sides. The doctor expressed serious doubts whether she would ever walk again. He warned that she would gain weight with the lack of exercise, and it would be emotionally frustrating as well. There would be anger and depression, he said. He wished us luck, but in his heart he felt the case was lost.

The family got together: my daughters flew in from Mumbai and Ahmedabad and we planned our strategy. We told Vimla that she would need to be in bed for four weeks only. We got a dietician to keep her weight in check and took turns in monitoring every morsel that she ate, for the one thing we could not afford was her gaining excessive weight. Now the task at hand was to fill in her time.

Again we scheduled our time in a way such that she was always occupied. We listened to music, meditated, chatted, saw movies together and sang. (She could sing considerably well as the part of the brain which controls this function is on the right, and her haemorrhage had been on the left. So, although she could not speak three words in a row, she could easily sing four to five lines). Since Vimla could not go to the club, the club came to our house: every evening friends and family gathered to chat and play cards.

Slowly the four weeks stretched to forty and Vimla was smiling when the doctor came to help her to her feet once again, this time after nine months. It was a historic moment for everyone in that house. Everyone had their eyes on her, but she had her eyes only on me. I stood a few paces away and asked her to come to me. At fifty-one she walked to me as a toddler walks to her mother. Everyone had tears in their eyes, but the doctor was astounded. 'This is a miracle!' he said.

Today it is twelve years since her haemorrhage. We go for our walks in the morning and spend our evenings at the club. Though the hours in between are still filled with endless therapies, life for us is beautiful.

Mahesh Killa

A Very Special Xmas Gift

Xmas has always been a time of joy and giving, of cheer and even miracles. As you grow up you stop believing in Santa, but there is always the anticipation of finding out what the little packets around the tree contain.

My Xmas gift came a day earlier and in the most unexpected way. I had gone to fetch Utpal from his boarding school and attend his PTA. His teacher handed me his results and as I read it I realised that this was undoubtedly the most beautiful Xmas present one could get. Fifty-seven on sixty were the marks he got and an appreciation that included the word 'excellent'. To some, my reaction would seem silly as Utpal is only four plus, but to those who know him and have followed the journey of his life, this piece of paper is much more.

What a story of survival it has been. Barely nine months ago Utpal lost everything that makes a child secure and safe to the demon of alcohol. He had no home, no mother, no extended family and no support. Previous to that fateful day in April 2006, he had survived third degree burns and lived a life where each evening meal and night's sleep depended on whether his mother had tippled nor not. Strange visitors, descents by cops and drunken brawls were usual occurrences.

When we found a school that would take him, there was an initial resistance: Utpal did not fit any mould, did not have the appropriate labels and social origins. But a young director took on the challenge and we waited with bated breath.

Six months and two school terms later, Utpal showed us what survivors are made of: he has a great support network in school ranging from the gently forbidding gatekeeper, to the class XII students and includes the hostel staff, the kitchen staff and even the principal. He still had one more point to prove, the one that rebuffs all the divisive policies that are kept on the boiler by dubious agendas and bear names like reservations or affirmative action. In the right environment, and with a peer group that cuts across social and economic backgrounds, little Utpal topped his class in an English medium boarding school.

Utpal was an ideal candidate for begging at a red light. Drunk parents, a nicely scalded body, and yet an incredibly beautiful face and endearing ways. A little help from Mr God, and friends who held on to our dream with us, made it possible for little Utpal to vindicate our resource centre.

As I hold his result sheet in my hand, I stand very tall and believe in miracles!

Anouradha Bakshi

Basama

The flyover close to where I live is lined with a small row of slum dwellings where around ten families reside. They have combined a few poles, plastic sheets and cloth to make homes, inside of which families—some of them comprising nine members—live alongside a few belongings. Whenever I pass by, I usually talk with the women and mess around with the children.

One day I was walking by when Hansaben, a woman who lost her legs and one arm in an accident, called me over. Although this woman sleeps on the fringes of roaring traffic and passes her days almost entirely alone, her face is always radiant. During many of our conversations, she proudly divulges that she studied till the fifth standard and repeats a few English phrases as a testament to the fact. She told me that, earlier in the day, she had seen a mentally challenged young woman wandering back and forth. She stopped her and learned that her name is Basama. Based on the way Basama's stomach protruded, Hansaben was worried that the girl might be pregnant. Basama spoke a language that no one could understand. In fact, one of the only things that everyone could understand was that this poor girl was hungry.

Hansaben and a few of the neighbours had taken the girl to a local restaurant that feeds leftovers to the homeless, but it had already closed for the afternoon. Basama, who appeared no older than eighteen, kept repeating that she wanted food. One of the other women and her eight-year-old son thought of a solution. They disappeared for some time and returned with kichadi after about an hour. They had spent the last hour begging for food to feed Basama.

Hansaben asked me to help Basama, especially since she was in such a delicate condition and no one could ensure her safety on the street. Hansaben's concern touched me. With the help of some good friends, we took Basama to a clinic, where the doctor confirmed that she was not pregnant. Her stomach had swollen due to malnutrition. We then registered a report at the police station and they admitted her into a mental institute. Since then we have visited Basama at the institute to check in on her and Hansaben always asks me about Basama. It continues to amaze and inspire me how, as little as Hansaben and the others in that community own, they were willing to give so much love to a girl they knew so little about.

Anjali Desai

Our Indian Idol

It's 9 p.m. in the little hill station of Shillong. The streets are deserted. The incessant rain which has flooded the Umiam Lake patters on tin roofs. I remind my mother that it's time for *Indian Idol*. The moment she switches on the television, the doorbell rings. Krishna, our Bengali neighbour, saunters in with his wife and their four-year-old daughter. My sister leaves her guitar and runs to the TV room while my father finally puts down the Jeffrey Archer he's been reading the entire evening. Krishna takes a cigarette and offers one to my father though his wife frowns at him. They light their smokes, settling down just as the signature tune of the show blares from the TV. This has become sort of a ritual for us ever since Amit Paul, a local lad, made his debut on *Indian Idol*—a Khasi family and a Bengali family watching a reality show together. You might ask, 'What's so special about that?' The fact is that Shillong has been ravaged by communalism over the years; Bengalis and Khasis rarely meet, let alone share a meal. That is, till Amit Paul happened.

It is an important round; two of the three remaining contestants will go on to the finals, and one will eventually be crowned the Indian Idol—the voice of a music-loving nation.

The first contestant goes on stage and sings his song, an old Bollywood number that sends the crowd into a frenzy. Young or old, all members of the television audience stand and sway to the music, clapping their hands and singing along with the contestant. The judges are pleased. My sister looks at mother as if to say, 'Can our Amit Paul do better than this?' Not sure whether our local hero will rise to the occasion, my mother calls up her sister during the commercial break.

'Did you hear him singing? Do you think Amit will sing something better?'

'I don't know but I don't think he can be better than our Paul.'

Finally our own *BahBah* (brother) Amit takes the stage. Spiked hair, red jacket and faded jeans, he picks up the microphone and starts singing an old classic—*Kora kagaz tha*. My sister can't take her eyes off him. Father apparently knows this song and he joins in the chorus. Krishna looks amused at how he mispronounces the Hindi words and pats him affectionately on the back. Once Amit's song is over the small crowd gathered in front of the TV goes wild, cheering 'Shillong, Shillong!' And everybody whips out their cell phones to sms on behalf of their favourite hero.

The equation is simple: the more votes for a contestant, the more his chances are of reaching the finals. Even the four-year-old has a toy phone with her and is sms-ing *'Mit.'*

Once the show is over, the others relax and chat, while my mother excuses herself to see to the preparations for dinner. The meal is served in a while and Krishna is rather concerned that mother has to trouble herself. 'No, no it's alright,' she says. 'We'll come home to your place for the finals; you can cook *mach* for us.' Everyone bursts out laughing.

The next day I am in a local taxi on my way to college. The taxis here are rather fancy I must admit. A music system always adorns the dashboard along with a plethora of CDs. Although they are like buses, since one has to share the vehicle with four other people, not many complain because they serve as a mode of transport and also as a mobile living room where passengers share *kwai* (beetle nut) and talk about politics, economy, sports and music (you cannot escape music when you're in Shillong). Lately, the economy, sports and politics has taken a backseat; Amit is the only reason one doesn't want to get off at his or her destination.

'Did you watch *Indian Idol* last night right? Hope you sms-ed on his behalf?' an old Khasi lady, whose teeth are stained red with *kwai*, asks me. I tell her I did, and just then the driver switches on his music system and plays *Kora kagaz tha*, one of the songs Amit sang last night. The other passenger, who happens to be a Bengali, blurts out in broken Khasi that he is planning to go and watch Amit perform live the moment he comes to Shillong. Soon everybody is exchanging numbers, arranging to meet on the day Amit performs in Shillong. I get down and wave goodbye. The remaining passengers, and the taxi driver, smile back. We've all just made new friends.

Shillong used to be a quiet and peaceful hill station. But from the early '70s, communalism began plaguing the town. Then came militancy, which further crippled it. Fortunately the tremors of militancy are starting to fade, and now, thanks to Amit Paul, this scourge of communalism is likely to be removed. Though he didn't manage to win the crown, he's done something far bigger—woven together disparate hearts. And we owe it to him to keep the music alive.

Jeffery D. Nongrum

Friends Forever

Ravale village was in the grip of terror: a leopard was attacking people in the vicinity and several human lives had already been lost. Cattle and dogs too had fallen prey to the silent stalker. As night descended, every villager lit a fire in front of his hutment to keep the marauding leopard away.

Little Ramnath watched the village elders huddled around the fire, faces grim with resolve, armed with wooden lathis and iron rods, waiting for the leopard to descend upon them. There was no telling when and where the animal would strike, unless they could lure him in and trap him . . .

Ramnath sensed the gravity of the situation. But with the childlike abandon of a six-year-old, he left the thinking to the adults and was soon involved in a vigorous game of catch with his friends. His adopted dog Moti was an equally noisy participant, chasing Ramnath around, and barking furiously at those who attempted to catch his little master.

The villagers soon decided how to catch the leopard. A stray dog would be tied to a stake at the outskirts of the village, as bait. Armed villagers would lie in wait for the bloodthirsty animal as it zeroed in on this easy target. It was the best solution. They decided to carry out their plan the following night.

Shambu had been given the task of setting the trap. As evening fell the next day, he had the squealing dog tied. A small sacrifice for a big victory.

On the other side of the village, Ramnath was distraught. Where had Moti disappeared? His bowl of roti and milk lay untouched, surely a bad sign. Neither was Heera there, nor Panna; in fact none of the scrawny army of animals that followed Ramnath around was to be seen!

Just then Raju came tearing up to the house and dropped the bombshell. Moti had been caught by Shambu and tied as bait for the leopard! Heera and the others were there already, wailing piteously. They needed help.

Soon Ramnath had rounded up a rescue brigade. Armed with nothing but love, they set out to battle the village elders. Moti yelped with delight as Ramnath flung his arms around his neck; Heera jumped in happiness. Hope was written large on their mute faces.

You cannot feed Moti to the leopard, or Heera or Panna . . . . Ramnath stood fearless in defence of his pets.

I love them, just as you love me, he told his father.

Would you tie me to the stake and watch me die?

The village elders had no answer; they had to capitulate. Another way would be found to get the leopard. Life was to be saved, not bartered.

Thankfully, the leopard was soon caught by forest guards, and no blood was shed.

Seven years have passed since. If you are in Ravale and happen to see a boy of thirteen in a white kurta pyjama and dark glasses, being led around by a small white dog, you will know them as Ramnath and Moti. Sadly, Ramnath lost his eyesight two years after the leopard incident. Moti devotedly plays guide and tries to repay the debt of love.

Vinita S.

Hariya

As is my habit, that morning too I stepped out onto our veranda to take in some air. Looking around, my glance fell on a bundle of green in a corner of the veranda. It was a parrot; its awkward twitching indicated that it was alive. Even as I approached it the parrot made no effort to fly away. Parrots are intermittent visitors to our veranda but always skitter away if you get too close to them. It was obviously wounded in some way. I picked it up.

By then I had been joined by my wife and children. Much was made of the unexpected visitor. My wife got her first-aid kit. It seemed to have some minor bruises but nothing of a serious nature. It allowed us to apply a gentle salve to its wounds.

The parrot ate some channa and drank some water. And made no effort to fly away.

I expect we named it Hariya because of its bright green plumage, and it became a family pet. A cage was bought more to protect Hariya from predators than to keep him imprisoned. In fact, we often let him out of his cage, so he could fly away if he wanted to. Hariya just didn't seem to want to. It was only after many days that we realised that he had never shown an urge to fly.

One day I took Hariya in my hands and gently examined him more thoroughly than we had ever done. To my horror I found that his wings had been stitched up with very fine plastic thread that was almost invisible to the naked eye. Someone had obviously taken great pains to ensure that Hariya couldn't fly.

Removing those threads was a very difficult task—it took me a whole week because it had to be done gently and slowly. It was only Hariya's faith and confidence in me that allowed it to happen. As I removed the last thread, Hariya squawked and fluffed his suddenly freed wings. Then his neck swivelled around and he just stared at me. Hariya's eyes seemed to be shining.

That day Hariya made no effort to fly. He flexed his wings often, but that was about it.

The next day we released Hariya from his cage. For a few minutes he just strolled around the veranda. Then suddenly he squawked the loudest we had ever heard him do, and as we watched, his wings flared and he was flying. Hariya soared into the air.

A few days later, when I walked out into the veranda for my morning stroll, I found Hariya perched on the railing. Seeing me, he flew up, squatted on my shoulder and rubbed his head on my cheek.

Hariya is now an intermittent visitor to our house, going and coming as and when he pleases. He often brings along a friend or two.

My wife says it is a relationship of a previous birth. My smallest child, just four years old, says it is love.

Purani Pinakin L.

How My Life Changed Its Course

Ever since I can remember, I always felt I was stupid, really stupid. I lost my father when I was three. Since I was a sick child, a polio victim, I lived with my grandmother in Mumbai so I could avail of the metro's advanced medical facilities. I remember being on the streets all day, playing or lazing around.

When I turned ten, my mother and my sister came to live in Mumbai too. My sister was a bright student, always securing high grades. She and my mother encouraged me to study, but I just could not bring myself to concentrate on any subject. I would get bored and feel sleepy when forced to open my books. After innumerable lectures on the importance of studying had failed, mother tried threats as well, but nothing worked. I truly believed I was stupid; no matter how much I worked, it wouldn't help.

One afternoon, as always, I was sitting under a tree in the school premises eating potato wafers when I saw a former classmate approaching me. Aditi and I had been in the same class the year before. I had failed sixth grade and had to repeat the year; Aditi had topped the class and was the brightest student of the seventh grade too. I flinched a little as I saw her walk towards me.

'Hi,' she said.

'Hi,' I replied, but not with much enthusiasm; I wanted her to leave. I continued to eat my chips.

Ignoring my coldness, she sat down next to me. For five minutes neither of us spoke and then she asked, 'Is Devika your real sister?'

'Yes, she is,' I answered.

'So how come she doesn't teach you so that you too can do well?' she asked. I peered at her, wondering if she was making fun of me, but all I could see on her face was earnestness. No, she is not trying to tease me, I decided. This time I answered a little more warmly, 'She tries to, but I don't like studying.'

'Why not? I'm sure you can get good grades too,' she said emphatically.

'No, I can't. I have no brains. God forgot to give me brains, health or beauty. He gave me nothing.'

'That's not true. And anyway, health and beauty can't be helped, but God has given brains to everyone, we only have to learn to use it.'

I shook my head, 'No, I have difficulty in concentrating, and books bore me; there is no hope for me. Please leave me alone. I am stupid, and always will be.'

With the gentlest tone that she could muster she said, 'I can prove it to you that you are not stupid. Give me one chance, I will teach you to study.'

Though I was softening from inside, I still held on to my low self-esteem. 'You'll be wasting your time. I cannot study, I am not as bright as you are nor as lucky as my sister,' I said.

'Let me try and help you, please. I will show you the right way to study. You just have to cooperate with me. Will you try?'

Her belief in me proved more powerful than my doubts about myself. She won and I relented.

For the next six months, she taught me patiently, before classes began, during lunch breaks, at times even after the day gave over. She made the subjects interesting, explained concepts, gave me home-work and religiously corrected what I'd done every morning. I developed the habit of reading, my concentration powers rose. When that term ended, I came fourth in my class!

Yes, she did prove to me that I had brains, but more importantly she taught me that if I put my mind to it, I could do anything I wanted.

Securing good grades brought me many privileges. I became my teachers' favourite pupil. For my part, I started enjoying classes. I received encouragement and respect from my teachers, and this made me try harder. As a result I did even better. While initially I was in a vicious downward spiral, now it seemed I was on an upward one … and all because of a peer who was interested enough and believed in a shy, uncommunicative girl!

Aditi and I kept in touch till we moved to separate colleges and eventually different cities.

I grew up and decided to be a teacher too. I went on to graduate, then did my postgraduate in teacher's training for special children. Today, I'm considered the smart one in the family!

As coordinator of a special school for the mentally challenged, I train children in certain skills. To what degree I succeed in imparting my skills to these children I don't know, but one thing I'm sure I succeed in, is in making them believe that, if they put their minds to it, they can do whatever they want.

I met Aditi recently, after a span of almost twenty-four years. I reminded her how her interest in me had changed the course of my life. She refused to take any credit; her words still ring in my ears, 'You were destined to find a guide Pushpa, I just happened to be the agent.'

I have no idea what made Aditi walk up to me that day, but I know that if I am proud of what I am today, it is because someone cared enough to make me believe that if I put my mind to it, I can do anything I want.

Pushpa Moorjani

Impervious to Love?

I always thought of myself as a strong person. Not in the physical sense of the word, but emotionally. I never quite understood what actually caused a boy to fall in love with a girl. Apart from some mild crushes, I had never really felt the pangs of love for any girl. I always believed I was impervious to love. My conservative Gujarati upbringing, along with my sensitivity towards my parents' feelings and expectations, never really allowed me to water the plant of feelings for girls who were not Gujarati-Brahmins. And, having stayed outside Gujarat for most of my teenage years, I didn't meet any girls with whom I could've permitted myself to fall in love. I almost prided myself on the fact that I couldn't fall in love with a girl. Until recently.

The company I work with required me to communicate with a client company in Bangalore. I began chatting with one of the girls there; soon, high-priority work required us to call each other once in a while. She came across as a friendly girl—a Tamilian, basically from Calicut, but brought up in Mumbai. It couldn't have been a more cosmopolitan upbringing. Before we knew it, we were constantly chatting to each other. We would wait impatiently for our chat ι indows to produce that 'click', signalling an incoming message, so we could read and reply . . . and then wait for the next reply . . . and so it went on, tirelessly. And before we knew it, if no sound came, or if the screen didn't blink for some time, it affected our mood. Much before we knew it, we were getting involved. Within a week of our first chat, she told me she had feelings for me.

I had not as yet thought about this. I was still under the impression that we were nothing but good friends. Years and years of self-imposed restrictions had never really allowed me to look at interactions with women as anything beyond the purview of friendship. And yet I found I was drawn to her; drawn like I had never been to any girl before. Getting to know her in that first week had been the most exhilarating and unexpectedly pleasant experience of my life. We began talking to each other at night. But it was not just about the conversation; it was the other's presence at the end of the line that mattered. Hanging up was suddenly the most difficult thing to do in the world. And yet I continued to hold on desperately to the belief that I hadn't fallen in love with a girl who was not a Gujarati. I was still trying to assure myself that there was an escape; there was still a way to avoid all the hassles I was going to plunge myself into. And yet, there was a desire to be wanted, to be loved by someone other than your parents and family.

During the course of our last late-night conversation, I failed to tell her unequivocally how I felt about her. Perhaps I hadn't decided. Perhaps I was being overcautious. Perhaps I wasn't ready for a commitment just yet. But I made her say the same thing scores of times. And she did repeat it, without expectations. Each time her words tingled my skin. And yet, I didn't realise how selfish I was being, making her profess the affirmation repeatedly. With each statement, I was plunging her into a deep valley, from which I myself would not be able to rescue her.

Then I told her a whole lot of things about my tastes, talents and women friends. She then realised she was different, different from the kind of girl I was looking for. She developed the —incorrect—idea that I was somehow better than her, more talented than her, and that I deserved a better girl than she. So, she decided to break it all on her own. She gracefully accepted the fact that it was not necessary for me to fall for her just because she had fallen for me.

She came into my life like a whirlwind. In a matter of a week, she made me realise I was not impervious to love, and these feelings could enter my fortress irrespective of caste, religion and other barriers I had built for myself. She pulverised the castle of my pride to dust with her gentle voice and friendly demeanour. She taught me that the character of a person is revealed not when relationships are made, but when broken. It is the grace with which she accepted our differences and the loss of the first love of her life that made her a much better person than I was.

We've scores of yardsticks to measure the success of a person. But the strength of a person lies in how gracefully he or she accepts failure. And we've failed to produce yardsticks for that.

I'm jealous of her. She had the courage to accept the situation and get to a depth of love without bothering about the consequences. She was brave enough to go right under the waterfall of love. I stood at the shore and dampened my feet with water. I was the loser on both counts. I lost my pride and am bereft of her love as well.

Kamlesh Acharya

My Magic Carpet

Five months pregnant and darting to work every morning, I was showing no signs of slowing down. One morning, at breakfast, my husband Jo suggested that we take some time off, go for a short holiday to London and prepare for parenthood by indulging in some baby shopping. I sensed that this was his sweet way of making me take some time off work and letting me indulge the way all mommies-to-be are allowed.

Before I knew it Emirates had flown us away and soon we were shopping on Oxford Street. On our third day there we visited our friends, parents of a two-year-old and our rich source of tips on parenthood. After exchanging hugs and kisses, our friends gave us a tour of their new home. While in their baby's room, I chanced upon a frame displaying a drawing of the little one's tiny feet. My maternal hormones went berserk. My friend informed me that the illustration was done by an old artist who lived some distance away from London. It was what she was planning to gift us when we had our baby. I don't remember anything that followed after seeing that masterpiece, not even the menu of the elaborate dinner that she had most enthusiastically laid out for us. All I wanted was to meet the artist and find out more about her work.

The very next morning I cajoled my husband to take me to visit the artist. He was a little reluctant, but gave in because, after all, the entire trip was about indulging me.

With a much pregnant belly, wearing a winsome smile, I marched towards the receptionist. I got a rude shock when I was told that it would not be possible to meet the artist without an appointment.

I couldn't be deterred however. Convincing Jo at breakfast the next morning, we once again taxied our way to Mrs Ferguson's studio. Despite sweet-talking the receptionist, I was coldly shown the door with a 'perhaps you should come once the baby is born'.

Jo tried his best to convince me that it would probably be best to return when we had the baby, but I guess he couldn't win the battle with my crazy surge of hormones. Back again on the third day we found ourselves in the reception area again. As much as he wanted to be the Invisible Man, my husband had to be there by my side.

By the fourth day, waiting endlessly in the studio, I had already converted the urge to get an impression of my baby into a business plan. I was sure that if the artist was so busy making memorabilia in a country where it was easy for parents to tell their children to find their own home when they grew up, I would have no problem setting up a similar business in India, where familial relationships are valued above everything else.

Finally, on our fifth visit, Jo managed to convince the receptionist to allow us a ten-minute meeting with Mrs Ferguson. The artist was completely unimpressed with my business proposal; she demanded a fee fat enough to buy a home in London. Jo was convinced that this was just to put us off. All through the journey back to the hotel we were silent. I didn't eat much at dinner and don't remember what breakfast was the next day . . .

Seeing my long face Jo tried to humour me with Gucci and Prada, but that's not what I desired, at least not this time! Here was an amazing business opportunity staring at me in the face, and I was pretty sure I could make a great success out of it. All I needed was Jo to have faith in my ability to do it even though the timing seemed wrong by conventional standards.

The next morning Jo sat in front of me on the breakfast table, ready for a discussion. He reasoned with me: it meant that I would have to stay back in London for six weeks, when I would be in the more difficult stages of my pregnancy. At this point, any husband might be justified in saying, 'Slow down sweetie! We have a baby coming, and that's going to mean a lot of settling down, sleepless nights. We really don't need any more on our plate right now!' And maybe I would have understood . . .

But seeing how enthusiastic I was, he relented. He agreed to go back alone and renegotiate the deal with Mrs Ferguson. His expression after the meeting told me that he had indeed cracked the deal.

I honestly do not know another man who would have given in. Isn't the stereotype that husbands will only remind their pregnant wives that giving birth, nursing and raising the baby is all that they should look forward to? All else—especially a new business venture—can most definitely wait. But not my husband! Always letting me be me; he had faith that I would neither neglect my baby nor my work.

Mrs Ferguson could not fight my knight and I stayed on in England to train in the very special art. I launched my business on the twentieth day after my daughter Tia was born. The portrait of her at one day old, taken on the hospital bed with Jo's help, was a showstopper at my launch and there has been no looking back.

Jokingly I refer to him as 'my magic carpet', the one that I can fly on and go *anywhere* I wish to . . .

Bhavna Jasra

No Bananas for My Mommy

A late call last night asked me to come and meet Utpal's mother who was in hospital with multiple problems including alcoholism. They asked me to bring Utpal along. So this morning, he wore his favourite T-shirt and we made the long journey to the hospital. On the way he spoke a little, asking time and again whether we were bringing her home. I told him that it would not be this time, as she was ill.

As we entered the hospital ward, he clung to me, and when he lay eyes on his mother he just looked away. In spite of her efforts he did not go into her arms but talked a lot and then took the camera and starting taking a lot of pictures. For a four-year-old the results were quite stunning, he even turned the lens and took one of himself!

Then he set off with Radhey, his friend and our driver, to get bananas and curds for his mom. While he was away the counsellor came and told me about the fact that Utpal's mom was being difficult and needed to be talked to as her health was poor and that she had to make efforts and get rid of her tantrums. That is when Utpal came back; he must have heard some of the conversation, or at least sensed the mood.

He said nothing and sat on a chair waiting for us to finish. When it was time to leave he just picked up the bag of bananas, saying that he was taking them back and after a quick forced hug for his mother he just walked away . . .

We dropped by the rehabilitation centre where I had a few matters to settle, and Utpal bonded with all the young counsellors, happily sharing his precious bananas and walking quietly into many more hearts.

On the drive back he fell asleep, his little head on my lap and I sat wondering, trying to make sense of what had happened. Perhaps it was simply Utpal's way of telling his mom that he had kept his part of the deal while she had not.

Utpal's mother has always been a difficult woman with too much attitude. I only hope she is able to understand what her son tried to tell her as best he could!

Anouradha Bakshi

Sharing

The drive back home seemed to take forever and the silence in the car was deafening. With me were my children, Aiyda and Abdullah, and my husband, Ayoub. We had just dropped my parents at the airport as their three-month sojourn with us had come to an end. Silently I watched the stars in the winter skies above . . . why is it so hard to say goodbye, I wondered.

With a small jerk, the car came to a standstill; I was home. As I turned on the lights, the gloom in my heart grew. I saw emptiness everywhere: in the hall, kitchen, corridor. No one spoke; we retired to bed hoping the ache would leave with sleep.

As I tossed and turned, restless in bed, I heard little sobs in the dark. I inched towards Aiyda only to meet a tight hug and a faint voice, 'When will we see them again?' Trying hard to fake a smile, I said, 'Soon sweetheart, very soon.' We talked about naniammi and nanu and how they were so special. Our chatter broke the silence in the house. Soon the boys in the house joined us. As I listened to them speak of the many things they would miss about my parents, I realised I was not alone. I had grown up a single child; sharing emotions was not something I understood well. All this time, I had been feeling the pain of separation without giving a thought to what the others were going through; or how much it would help to share our feelings. I had shut myself away from them, as they tried to respect my feelings with silence. Suddenly, my loneliness seemed so small.

Aiyda said she would miss the tickling sessions she had with naniammi; Ayoub would miss having my father around to chat with; Abdullah would miss going to the park with his grandparents; and I . . . well, I would miss them for every second they have been with me. We talked and talked and talked about them till we could talk no more. My children fell asleep in my arms. Ayoub returned to bed.

Once again there was silence, but this time it was different. A sense of satisfaction took over the gloom. The children had grown up so fast, they knew how to care. They understood the words I could not say. I felt a smile curl up my lips. I closed my eyes and let the last tear roll down my cheeks.

Ruqya Khan

Talking of Love

Over the phone, he said,
My wife died two years ago.
I understand, I said.
I lost mine years back . . .
It still hurts. Yes, he said.

For all that bigness
He was like a lost child.
As soon as was decently possible
I took him into my arms,
and for the first time
he was able to talk about death
And not weep. For the first time
I was not bitter about my loss.

Two hurts together
Cancel each other out,
or so it seems.

Jane Bhandari

Unspoken Contract

'Where to?' the rickshaw driver asks me with his mouth full of tobacco. 'Vijay Char Rasta,' I say. I'm headed to meet Sampat, Raj and Archana to talk about the purpose of life and things like that.

After some light conversation, the rickshaw driver and I quickly become friends. 'Are you from Ahmedabad?' he asks me. 'No, I'm just visiting a friend.' 'Just a visit?' 'Yes, he's opening a restaurant and he wanted my parents to inaugurate it. I'm helping him launch the café.'

'Café? You mean it's like a Barista?' he asks, displaying his knowledge of the trendy coffee joints in town. 'No, not quite like Barista,' I say. 'It's called the Seva Café. It's a place where everyone is a volunteer and no one gets charged for their food. It's going back to our roots, where each person is treated as a part of you, and not a customer: Atithi Devo Bhava. We start each relationship by giving, and not by thinking of receiving.'

The rickshaw driver progressively gets more and more blown away as I continue to talk about the 'Pay-it-Forward' model. 'I can't believe that such a thing can exist in a world like this. Today everyone is after money. No one gives.

Corruption is everywhere, even in our government. The world needs more people like your friend.'

'What's your name, by the way?' I ask the pumped-up rickshaw driver. 'Mohan,' he answers. 'Don't call me "kaka" (uncle); I'm like your brother. Call me Mohanbhai.'

When I press him a bit about his own life, Mohan starts talking about his bad habits. 'Sahib, what can I say? It's hard. I know it's bad for me, I've seen all the tobacco-related cancer patients in the hospitals but it's hard to let it go.' I suppose we're all in the same boat with our bad habits, but Mohan has got honesty working for him.

In between the loudly honking horns and the exceptionally noisy rickshaw, Mohan drives slowly at the side of street so we can converse. He even starts reciting some poems in praise of human virtue.

'How long have you been in Ahmedabad?' I ask. He says, 'My whole life. We used to have a farm in our village, but now I just drive a rickshaw. It's good money.' 'About how much money do you make every day?' 'Oh, two to three hundred rupees. It's really good.'

This is one thing I've noticed—people with more money are more self-conscious about it. I can't imagine any of my middle or upper class friends volunteering information about their exact salary.

Thus far, our conversation has been in pure Gujarati. And then, out of nowhere, he says, I'm a B.Com graduate. I speak English.' I'm taken aback. And then he reads aloud a couple of the English billboards, happily bragging about his skills. A college graduate driving a rickshaw? 'Oh yes, this way I take home about three thousand rupees a month for my family. Nothing else gives me that kind of money,' Mohan explains.

'How many people in your family?' 'Two daughters, one son and my wife,' he says with a smile as he describes his loved ones.

By now, Mohan and I are almost brothers in service: I am excited to be given a window into his life, and he is enthralled by the heroic experiment of my friend's Seva Café.

Soon, my fourteen-minute rickshaw ride comes to an end. It is time for me to pay. 'How much?' I ask. He checks his meter and says, 'Twenty-three rupees.'

I look in my wallet and notice that I have two hundred and forty rupees; the sum he earns every day on an average. Spontaneously, I say, 'Mohanbhai, here's two hundred and forty rupees. Will you drive your rickshaw in the Seva Café style today?'

A moment of stunned silence.

I explain, 'For the rest of the day, tell your customers that someone else before them has paid their bill for them, and if they want to continue the chain of kindness, they can contribute whatever they want. See what happens.'

Mohan is awestruck. Shaking his head in disbelief, he says, 'No sir, no sir, I can't take this.' 'Why not?' I ask. 'No, no, sir, you don't understand. I'm a terrible guy. How do you know I won't just take the money and run?'

'Mohanbhai, if I didn't trust you, why would I give you the money?'

'Sahib, don't trust me. I'm a very bad person. No one trusts me,' he says. He goes on, and I interrupt his tirade with a one-liner and an extra-broad smile on my face: 'Too late. I already trust you.'

Again a moment of stunned silence. Mohan doesn't exactly know what to do.

'Okay sir, tell me your name. I will come and tell you exactly what happened with this money.'

'It's okay, Mohan. I already trust you fully. You don't need to tell me anything. It will be an unspoken contract between you and the world,' I say.

Still, Mohan feels a need to reassure me that he will live up to the faith I have placed in him. After fumbling around for a bit, he gathers money from all his pockets. 'See, see, I have three hundred and twelve rupees on me. You have given me two hundred and forty. I will do my honest best today. You can be sure of that. I won't let you down.'

It's hard not to be elated after such encounters. Rupees two hundred and forty is about the price of two movie tickets; no movie has ever left me feeling this enthused about life.

Just as I am about to leave, Mohan says, 'Sahib, I won't let you go without taking your name and address.'

'Mohan, I'll tell you what. You and your family, you come to the Seva Café some day. You've seen the Reebok building; it's right on the fourth floor. If you come in next week, I'll be your waiter. Otherwise, ask for Jayeshbhai and tell him you're my friend. He'll know.'

Mohan grabs a newspaper that was tucked near his seat, pulls out a pen and writes down a few things in Gujarati. 'One day, bhai, I will find you and tell you all my stories.' Almost silently, he whispers, 'Thank you.'

'See you, my friend,' I say, walking off. He smiles, snaps his fingers and lifts his right index finger towards the sky. I'm not sure what he means, but sense that it is perhaps a seal on our unspoken contract.

Nipun Mehta

When Tina Met Santa

Tina wanted to see Santa Claus. She had seen him in movies, read about him in storybooks and had heard about him in songs. Now she wanted to see him in person. And more than anything else, she wanted to shake his hand. That would tell her whether he was real.

When she told her father about her wish, he took her to Hill Road that very evening. Hill Road was a haven for Christmas shoppers and an unusual place for a Hindu father and daughter to be at on Christmas Eve. But Tina's father knew that Santa Claus would be visiting one of the stores.

Tina was mesmerised. The shiny tinsel balls, the shimmering fairy lights and the beautiful, sparkling Christmas trees took her breath away. The store was like a fairyland. Families were filling up wooden baskets with their last minute shopping. Mothers and fathers were selecting figures for their nativity scenes. Little girls were squealing in delight at the sight of angels dressed in gold and white. Little boys were inspecting toy drums or nibbling on striped peppermint-flavoured candy cane.

Tina looked into her father's eyes. At once, each knew what the other wanted. Tina's father held her hand. 'Buy whatever you like,' he whispered.

Tina was still quite little, but she knew that this was a very expensive store. And of late, she had often heard her mother say that her father wasn't bringing home as much money as he once had.

She wondered whether buying something would be wise. Or right. She looked at her father again. Again, she knew that his eyes mirrored exactly what was in his heart.

Tina decided to make a careful selection. She picked up the smallest Santa doll, a small box of star-shaped marzipans, and a pair of hair clips shaped like Christmas trees. She hoped they weren't very expensive and that they would make her Christmas very bright.

Pleased, both father and daughter walked hand in hand and waited with the other shoppers for Santa Claus. It was then that they saw the girl enter the store.

She was almost Tina's age. Her face was caked with mud and her hair was long and unkempt. You could tell that the tattered clothes she was wearing weren't her own. They were far too large for her. The girl didn't have shoes and Tina kept wondering how the girl's father had allowed her to walk barefoot on the cold and grimy roads.

The more Tina looked at the girl, the more she thought she knew her. The girl's face was full of wonder. Tina knew that she had seen the face before. On the shiny, silvery tinsel ball she had so closely looked at when she had first entered the store. The girl was just like her. She too wanted to revel in the Christmas spirit and catch a glimpse of Santa.

'Shoo!' a voice said rudely. A security guard appeared and drove the girl out of the store, as though she was an unwelcome fly. The girl's face now looked crestfallen. But she turned around and did exactly as told.

Father and daughter looked into each other's eyes again. Once again, each knew what the other wanted. Quietly, Tina walked up to the girl and slipped the paper bag into her hands. The girl was speechless. Too shocked, too delighted to say anything. She clutched the paper bag and ran to rejoice under the light of a street lamp.

Suddenly, a loud cheer broke out. Tina saw that Santa Claus had arrived. He was exactly as she had imagined. Jolly and rotund, with a flowing white beard, and twinkling eyes. Santa Claus saw Tina. He bent down and put his hand out. 'Merry Christmas!' he said. 'Merry Christmas,' Tina replied softly, without shaking Santa's hand.

'What happened?' Tina's father asked, after they had left the store, 'I thought you wanted to shake Santa's hand.'

'I was holding it all evening, Daddy.' Tina said softly.

Father and daughter looked into each other's eyes again. And they both saw the magic of Christmas.

Pooja Lulla

The Potter and the Clay

'He is going to be in your class. You should be careful—he should have been thrown out of school a long time ago.' There she stood, petite, thin, pretty, listening to the words of her seniors, teachers more experienced than she, far older than her thirty-something. She looked at them and inwardly sighed . . . another child had been turned into a monster by those very persons in whose care he had handed over his soul . . . his teachers.

She walked into the classroom; large, airy, desks neatly lined up in three rows, the plaque above the door reading 9A. She smiled as she saw that there was not a child sitting on the benches . . . no, children *must* sit on desks! Oh, how this rattled those old ladies in the Staff Room below! She chuckled to herself. Silently she stood at the door, and suddenly, as though of one mind, they scrambled off their desks and rushed to sit quietly in their seats, looking at her, some fearfully, some quizzically. None knew what to make of her. As juniors they had experienced her as the Head of Discipline, as seniors they had heard from the others that 'only the lucky ones get to go to her class'. Could the ex-students be right? They would find out . . . oh yes, they had two years in which to find out.

She stood silently before them, serenely looking at each teenager sitting before her, smiling at those she had worked with earlier, nodding gently at those she did not know yet. In each one's eyes she looked for something . . . . Had eight years of so-called 'discipline' by teachers already scarred the soul? Had the years robbed the soul of its self-esteem, of its self-honour, of its joy of being all that it was? And in all she saw that the horrible task was done. The teachers had been successful . . . for in every eye she could only see fear and distrust, not thrill and excitement. She sighed heavily, but she knew that again she was in the right place, at the right time. She had thirty beautiful souls to commune with, to awaken, to make them remember the god who lay dormant, but not dead, within them.

Crash! The door slammed open breaking the silence, and in skid Surya. Ah! Here he is! The 'monster'! Not much of a monster to look at, though. The class almost stopped breathing . . . first day of the new school year, and already Surya had a late mark against his name . . . now what? She knew this was the critical moment; if she lost this moment she may not find another one for a long time. She indicated that Surya remain standing by the door, and then proceeded to tell the class about the school elections that they would soon be competing in, and the responsibility that this involved. Then she asked the contenders to talk briefly of the posts they wished to campaign for.

Slowly she turned towards Surya, and he loudly, defiantly, stared back at her and said, 'School Games Captain'. She held his stare, although with his immense height and build, he towered over her. 'No, Surya, you are not eligible for these elections. I do not accept your nomination.' The class gasped. Did she not know that this was invitation for Surya to retaliate, to attack? 'Surya, there is only one qualification that is essential for these elections. Self-discipline. You and I will spend this year learning self-discipline, and next year, you will campaign for the post of . . . Head Boy.' This time the gasp was even louder. Head Boy? The most coveted post in school? Surya? Was she mad? Her statement, spoken with so much conviction, silenced even Surya, who had opened his mouth to shout at her. He looked at her in disbelief. Surely she was mocking him! But the smile that had lit up her face was so genuine he did not know what to do . . . but he knew he would do whatever she wanted, for somewhere within Surya, his soul had leapt up in acknowledgement, acknowledgement of its own will and authority. She had seen him for what he truly was, and in her face was acceptance, not rejection. Tears came to his eyes, and he looked away . . . no one would see him cry! No way . . . he, Surya, made others cry!

One year went by and slowly but surely Surya learnt self-discipline. He learnt to respect himself each time she gave him a task which he performed ably; he learnt punctuality each time he saw the gentle disappointment in her eyes when he entered late; he learnt consideration for others and faith in himself each time she wordlessly patted his shoulder in encouragement when he was sure he would fail; he learnt the pride of making a mistake and using it to succeed, each time she said 'I am sorry', knowing neither shame nor humiliation; he learnt love and perseverance each time she refused to give up on him or any other student in the class.

By the end of the year the talk in the Staff Room had changed considerably. 'Surya has improved so much. He is scared of you, that's why he does not dare to misbehave.' She smiled, for she and Surya both knew, as did all of 9A, that fear does not have the power to bring about transformation. Only love and acceptance do.

Yes, many teachers believe that discipline can be taught through fear and harshness. Fear creates the monsters that lie within the teacher's own heart; love gives birth to the god-child within. The soul is the divine clay in the potter's hand, and the potter can only create what he can see within himself.

Class 10A waited in eagerness for the results to be announced. They had all voted for Surya as Head Boy. But would the rest of the school? Would the student body only remember who he had been, and not recognise who he had become now? Just then she entered the class, her face beaming with pride and love, the tears of joy flowing freely down her cheeks. Simultaneously the Principal's voice was heard over the public announcement system: Head Boy . . . Surya Nagpal! The class erupted in a tumult of exultation. They hugged Surya, pummelled him in pride, held him up. She smiled. They were not only rejoicing Surya's victory, but their own . . . for when even one soul reclaims its power, other souls experience the fullness of their own divinity.

The students did not notice her leaving silently, once again thanking the Divine Power for making her a teacher . . . one who teaches a soul how to reclaim its power and use it for the good for all. She smiled at her naïvety, for as she walked down the stairway, she imagined that she heard the angels whisper 'Hallelujah'.

Ellaeenah

My Father, On Giving

For in truth, it is life that gives unto itself, while you,
who deem yourself a giver, are but a witness.

Kahlil Gibran, *The Prophet*

One of my favourites from Khalil Gibran's *The Prophet* are the lines on giving, where he says that the trees don't ask whether we deserve their fruits but we often say, 'We will give but only to the deserving'.

My father was one of the most generous persons I have known in my life. He used to give openhandedly to relatives, friends and strangers. He would tip very generously too. Once, on leaving the hospital after a cataract operation, he was tipping the nurses bigheartedly as usual. One of the nurses had been very ill-behaved and rude. Since my father's eyes were bandaged he didn't know whom he was giving the money to. I whispered, 'Don't give her so much money Appa.' He just silenced me with a gesture of his hands. Later he said, 'Never stop someone else from giving.' I was in school then, but till date the lesson has stayed with me.

He also had the habit of welcoming each and every salesperson into the house and buying something from them. It didn't matter what they were selling; clothes, gadgets, jewellery, crockery. He never forgot to offer them water too. Sometimes it was very annoying, but he always taught us compassion: one salesperson was too old, one too young, the other seemed tired: on some pretext or another everyone would be invited in.

Years later, when I was married, I gave up my full time job and joined a company which allowed me flexible working hours. The company dealt in encyclopaedias and high quality books and programmes for young children. It was one of the first and biggest companies in direct sales, a relatively new concept in India at that point.

Starting with friends and family and getting a positive response from them, I was motivated to visit strangers. 'Cold calling' is something which most people are terrified of in sales. So was I. But to my great surprise, people I visited were welcoming, generous and extremely warm. I met a lot of people, formed great friendships and got a lot of sales. I progressed very fast to the level of manager for the whole state of Gujarat. All my colleagues wanted to know the secret of my success, especially with 'cold calling'. I really didn't think much about it then.

But very recently, when I was buying something from a lady at the door, I remembered how my father always welcomed salespeople into the house. And I knew that it is to him that I owe my good fortune at 'cold calling'.

Anasuya Adhikari

Life Is Too Short to Be Small

One, as it turned out, not very fine morning, as I was sending both my children to school, our servant Ramlal came up to me. His normally cheeky, smiling face wore an unusually worried expression.

'Madam.'

'Just a minute, Ramlal. Aniruddh, don't lose your sharpener again! Bye, both of you . . .'

'Bye, Mom!' they screamed in unison and ran out.

'Yes Ramlal, what's the problem?'

'Madam, is Anilsaab sleeping in the downstairs room?' he asked, referring to my husband.

'No, of course not. He's gone to the gym.'

'But Madam, I went to clean the room and the door's not opening. I knocked several times and there's no answer. Someone's sleeping inside like Kumbakaran! With the door locked.'

We are a joint family of twelve living in the house, but we all sleep on the upper floors. The room Ramlal was referring to is never used as a bedroom. And the room is never, ever locked.

'Find out who is there, Ramlal, and let me know.'

After dressing, some fifteen minutes later, I remembered the locked room. Ramlal had not returned. I decided to go downstairs myself and investigate.

Walking down the stairs I saw a whole crowd of my domestic staff assembled in the passage outside the room.

'Ramlal, what is going on? Who was in the room?'

'Madam, it has to be Anilsaab in there. Everyone else is in their own rooms, getting ready.'

'Don't be silly! He's gone to the gym.'

Our driver, Tej Singh, who normally knows if anyone has left the house, piped in: 'Madam, Anilsaab hasn't gone anywhere.'

The first thing to cross my mind was, could Anil really be in there? The previous night I had been preoccupied with a problem of mine and had been very uncommunicative. I tried the door myself. It didn't open. I went out into the garden, and tried the other door and windows, but they were all locked. They always were. A thought made its way into my by-then disturbed mind. Someone I knew had recently committed suicide. I didn't think my husband would ever take his own life, but perhaps in certain circumstances, one can't really think practically?

I was getting more anxious by the minute. I knew that Anil would not have taken his cell phone with him if he had gone to the gym, and I was in no state of mind to look for their landline numbers. I called Anil's friend, Shreyans, but he had not gone to the gym that day. By then some of the other members of the family had started arriving.

Everyone seemed convinced it was Anil inside that room. Some were looking at me with sympathy, some had disapproving expressions on their face. I was going completely out of my mind.

'Just get the keys and unlock the door!'

'This door has no lock—it has a latch.'

'Get a screwdriver!'

Someone got a screwdriver, but it wouldn't go through the narrow space between the door and its frame.

'Break the door down!' I screamed.

Ramlal and Tej Singh attacked the door with their shoulders. It was to no avail. Ramlal then kicked near the handle and there was a sound of breaking wood. He kicked again and the door flew open.

We all streamed in.

The room was empty.

The handle had gotten stuck.

Tears of relief and happiness flew unashamedly down my face. All through those minutes that the door had stayed stuck, I had rebuked myself for being mean to my husband the previous day. I had wondered whether I would ever get a chance to tell him I was sorry, whether I would be able to go on without him. I realised then that I am because he is. He is not just a part of me, we are not two parts of a whole, but, as I realised in those frightening moments, he is me. These were not some clichéd feelings from a film, but my precise emotion at the time.

I ran up to my room and cried my heart out. I had only heard about tears of happiness till that day.

Soon enough Anil entered the room, laughing, most amused about what had happened. I rushed up to him and hugged him tight.

Seema Agarwal

The Unfolding Experience

The soul walks not upon a line, neither does it grow like a reed.
The soul unfolds itself, like a lotus of countless petals.

Kahlil Gibran, The Prophet

I cannot really say when it all started. For I do not know from where the winds arose, or who lit the flames in my sun.

This was a few years back when I had left for the United States from India to study at a prominent college and then pursue a career. At a professional level, one could say that I had done well as a young woman in a foreign country. I also had a decent social circle. There were many physical comforts and privileges that money could buy.

But somewhere, there was a strange kind of emptiness engulfing me all the time. I sometimes felt like a bird entangled in a kite string. There was a pain inside but no emotion to name it. There was unrest in the mind and a futility in the body. At times it felt as if all of reality was staring blankly, straight into my eyes.

This void did not seem to be caused by external circumstances. It seemed to emerge from somewhere deep inside me. Everything appeared very limited and measurable. There were days that made me question how we are born, how our lives get conditioned, how we struggle, compare, compete and one day vanish. Just like that! We strive for degrees, jobs, relationships, money, name and fame, and then one day we die. The whole of existence dissolving into the silence of space. Cycles of pain-pleasure-pain follow us like seasons of nature. An ever-changing insecurity; an uncertainty where every moment is a transition point only for another to take its place. How are we supposed to live this life? Where do we ultimately go?

As time passed, these questions became so irrepressible that I could see only two paths ahead of me. Either I go into this in a radical way and examine myself as sincerely as possible. Or follow the second path—death. There really was no other way. No escape. For now I had started seeing how I had escaped for the past twenty-five years of my life. I had used up all the emergency exits by now. I had experimented with a few extremes in my life and everywhere I had hit a wall. So now the only place left for me to go was within!

After some time I quit my work. I stayed home and spent many days alone in silence.

Somewhere, my faith in life had still not left me. There was a part of me that believed that life *is* fair. That was the foundation of my journey from the known to the nameless. I thought that if life was really fair, then we are not supposed to go through even a trace of suffering. We should be equipped with all that we need to live a life that is absolutely happy and peaceful, that is good for us and good for others.

In the period that followed, the inquiry only got more intense. There was an unknown force fuelling my search. I was travelling to places within myself that were never visited

before. I felt like, for the first time in my life, I was looking at
the naked beauty of my soul.

In this time, silence helped. There is something deeply
sacred about silence. I felt that when I was truly *alone*, I was
one with all.

Obviously, this pilgrimage within oneself is endless. But I
started feeling more awake than ever before. And a day came,
when it felt like the heart broke open. Something totally illogical
came over me. I felt like I was holding on to the moment like
a butterfly in my fist. Slowly the fingers uncurled and the
moment fluttered away like a colourful bird into a free sky.

Most things I had done in my life were all measurable and
calculated. Almost everything was only to benefit myself. But
now I had to do the exact opposite and see what happened. I
wanted to be illogical and unreasonable. And the most illogical
thing I could do was give without getting anything in return.
It was like setting free irrational acts of kindness and senseless
acts of beauty into this world. It was like writing poetry in the
prose of life. It was like allowing the inner universe to dance.

My world started changing dramatically. I started sharing
the skills that I would earlier charge thousands of dollars for,
completely free. I started volunteering for long hours with
different non-profits. In the year that followed, my
experiments took me to places I could have never imagined. I
cleaned public bathrooms and collected trash with the women
who did rag-picking for a living. I ate food with the homeless,
spent time with the terminally ill, painted with the mentally
challenged, danced with the young and the old, and shared
insights with complete strangers.

Now, love was no more a temporary sense of pleasure or
comfort. Love was emptying my entire being—and offering
the whole of myself. It was breaking open every barrier in the
heart so that generosity could flow.

Suddenly I started seeing the homeless man on the street
as my own brother. It felt that in some strange way, my own

happiness was tied to his wellbeing. It felt as if, by serving him, I was facing my own fears, aversions, and in some inexplicable way, healing a part of my own soul. I realised that the only way for me to make myself complete was to share with others unconditionally. In this fine tapestry of life, all strands are entwined to each other. In the larger whole, our lives are intrinsically connected, and in order for me to be truly happy I have to serve those who are suffering. I believe that service is an opportunity for us to become whole again.

Today service for me is not something that is limited to a certain section of society. Working in the slums of India or even listening to someone with complete attention can be an act of love. What service teaches me is that every single moment is filled with divine compassion and goodness and the more I am alive to it, the more I affect the world around me in a positive way. It is really about learning to experience the small ordinary moments of purposelessness.

Anonymous

What Matters Most

I grew up in Pune in a very normal family. The thing I liked most was being allowed to open the big cupboard where all the 'special' objects were kept lovingly by my mother. There were some china cups from England, a doll that we loved to look at but were not allowed to play with, a beautiful crystal bowl. They were very lovely, but we always kept them in the cupboard for the fear that they would break.

Many years later I got married. My husband was in the Army and so we would shift often. In every house, I would unpack the most beautiful and fragile things we had been given at our wedding, and carefully put them into a glass-fronted cupboard.

One day, when another Major's wife was visiting, and I had gone into the kitchen to make the tea, her son opened the cupboard. He was attracted by the willow pattern plates, a gift from one of my best friends. Just as I came out of the kitchen holding the tray, I saw him try to take one plate out. Not only did it smash into pieces, it brushed against some of the small glass figurines I loved very much—a swan and a tortoise—and those broke also.

Mrs Major apologised for her son, and what could I say? I had to put a smile on it, even though inside I felt terrible.

When my husband came back that night, he found me in tears. I had spent hours trying to put the plates and figurines back together with Araldite, but they were smashed beyond repair. I couldn't stop crying.

I told him the whole story, and he listened sympathetically. But I will never forget what he said next. 'Parul,' he said, 'many years ago, I heard someone say this and it helped me. I hope it will help you. Never cry over something that can't cry back over you.'

That stopped my tears. From all the places I had been to as an army officer's wife, what I remembered was not the houses or the beautiful things that other wives had, but their smiles and their warmth. People mattered. People were worth crying over. Not plates and glass statues.

Parul Mehra

2

ON PARENTING

We *worry about what a child will become*
tomorrow, yet we forget that he is someone
today.

Stacia Tauscher

Another Mountain to Climb

Leela, my almost one-year-old baby, is obsessed with climbing. Her discovery this morning—climb into the dishwasher, pull out the top rack, hang on it, and try to figure out how to climb on top of it.

She climbs on all the chairs, and has figured out how to get into the bathtub by positioning the stool so she can use it to climb several levels. She is on a mission to discover and climb onto whatever is in her world. She falls, she gets up and starts climbing again.

Tara, at the same age, was the complete opposite. She had no desire to move or be on top of things. Tara was always the quiet observer. She took all the information in, contemplating its meaning and significance. She would quietly sit in my lap, and want me to read one book after another to her. With Leela, if we get through two pages it is a feat! My little explorer cannot sit still for a moment.

If there was ever a lesson that we all come into this world with a different purpose and a unique soul, my children teach it to me every day!

Mallika Chopra

Baby Trilogy

1
To the Baby in My Womb

I don't know
your name—
yet.
I haven't looked into
your eyes
or smiled at
your smile.
But the very
instant,
the very
moment,
I saw your
black-and-white
tadpole-like figure
swimming on the screen,
I blinked away
tears

of a strange new love.
Immediately,
I grew ten pairs of arms
so that I could cuddle you,
protect you,
clothe you,
feed you,
warm you.
I sprouted eyes at the back
of my head
so that I could
watch you,
follow you,
gloat over you,
worry over you,
cry over you,
for you,
with you.
And immediately,
my heart grew larger
and larger
so that I could store
this strange new love
I felt for you.

I don't know
your name –
yet.
But my heart
is full to bursting,
with this strange new love
that you
have given birth to.

2
The Day Before

The day before;
I sit here
And wonder
will I laugh
or cry
when I see you
for the first time.
I wonder
who you'll look like
and maybe even love more—
your father or me?
I wonder
about your first smile,
your first step,
your first word.
I wonder
about your dreams
and whether they'll be the same as
the ones I dream for you.
I think
about they way you kick
as I write these lines
and the wonder I felt
the first time you kicked
and how,
after tomorrow,
I won't feel those kicks again.

The day before,
I sit here
in wonder
and wonder

how tomorrow,
you
will change
my life
forever.

3
At Last I Know

Here you are.
At last.
Here,
in the world.
Here,
in our home.
Here,
in my arms.

And now,
I finally know
your name,
your face.

But I also know more
than I ever
thought I would.
I now know
the smell of innocence.
I now know
the touch of purity.
I now know
what it is
to hold
a piece of my heart
in my hands.

I now know
the value
of a ten-minute snooze.
I also know
those peaceful nights
of slumber
are a thing of the past.

But the single,
most important thing
is that
at last,
after nine months
of waiting
and wondering,
I now know
you.

Baisali Chatterjee Dutt

I Am What I Am

My parents believed in me right from the beginning. I could share my feelings, doubts and anxieties with my father, however trivial or profound, with the faith that he would not judge me or tag me as wrong or right. I knew that I had an attentive and a willing ally in him, as well as a mentor who would guide me and handle my delicate feelings.

My father was in banking and so we often moved cities. During one such transfer, when I was in Class 6, I had to join a school in a new city mid-term. I had been given a double promotion in the third standard and was generally looked upon as a bright student in most schools that I had attended, but here a shock awaited me. After a half hour interview with the principal, I got the distinct impression that he was not impressed with me. He granted me admission more as a favour than on my academic merits. This upset me terribly.

On my way back home, my father read my mood and asked me, 'What is it, son?'

Since the principal had, after all, given me admission, my reservations about how he had judged me could have well been looked upon as silly or unnecessary. But I knew that my feelings were as important to my father as they were to me. I told him how I felt about the interview, and, after listening to me patiently and with complete attention, he said, 'Yes, maybe the principal did think less of you than what you would have wanted him to think, and this must be upsetting, but does this make you any less of the person you are? The reality is what you are, not his perception of you. You have created a perception in his mind in the half hour that you had, and maybe you could have created a better impression. But you have ample opportunity to work on it and change it to what you think is more deserving of you. But whether you succeed in doing so or not, it still does not change *you*.'

From that time on, I knew that irrespective of what people think of me, I am what I am. 'I' don't change because of an impression people might have of me.

Sanjeev Kapoor

Letting Go

There was joy and there were tears. My husband and I were at the airport, seeing our younger son off to university in the UK. Our elder son had flown the nest five years ago and was now settled in England. Now the little one was going too. The airport—with its bright lights and teeming travellers—was hardly the place to burst into tears, so I fought for self control. I tried to smile brightly and chatter on about the wonderful experience awaiting our boy. Like any good Indian, I was delighted with his admission into Cambridge University; but my pride in him was tempered by the prospect of the empty nest, and the loneliness that accompanies it.

The flight was announced. There was but time for a final, tight hug. Karan sensed the tears before he saw them. Relax mother, he comforted, it's only three months till Christmas break, time will fly. And you can come whenever you want—it's only nine hours away.

I let the tears flow as his retreating back became a distant speck. I cried the whole way back to the empty house. My husband picked up my son's refrain: it's only a question of three months, of nine hours, you can speak to him everyday, and so on and so forth.

We reached home. Moist-eyed I waited for the elevator to our flat. No more blaring music, I thought to myself, no sudden requests for mango milkshake, no more incessant stream of visitors, or the pleasant sound of young laughter.

'What is the matter, young lady?'

I looked up to find Mr Kapadia from the eighteenth floor. At eighty-five, he addressed all the women in the building as young ladies. Love to talk to pretty girls, he would say, though the prettiest one I ever knew abandoned me a decade ago. It was apparent that he still missed his late wife, Farida; he never missed the opportunity to pull out his wallet and show us her photograph.

'Just dropped Karan to the airport and am already missing him,' I replied sheepishly, as we went up in the lift.

'Ah, the pain of separation! Cheer up, young lady, your lad will be back before you know it,' Mr Kapadia consoled, as the lift stopped at his floor.

'Where is Freny today?' I had suddenly realised that the nurse who constantly accompanied Mr Kapadia was missing and the old man was groping in his pocket for the house keys.

'On leave. Her father had a stroke, she had to rush home,' was his matter of fact reply.

'Are you sure you are fine alone?' my husband asked, as he helped Mr Kapadia open the door and switch on the lights.

'I will be fine, thank you,' he replied, and we said goodbye.

'Spunky old man,' observed my husband. 'Must be tough being so alone.'

'Yes, it must,' I replied, suddenly overcome by remorse at how self-absorbed I was being.

Jolted out of my stupor, I thought, I must send Mr Kapadia some chicken makhani, he loves it. Somehow, I did not feel sorry for myself any more.

Karan called when he landed at Heathrow. The flight had been great he said, except they had served butter chicken that was not remotely like the one I make . . .

Marks and Spencer does a great microwave-friendly chicken tikka masala, I teased. It is only a question of three months . . . .

I still shed tears when saying goodbye to my boys. Missing them is part of motherhood.

But then, so is letting go.

Vinita S.

Overcoming Fears

Yesterday, at swimming class, my four-and-a-half year old daughter Tara was nervous about putting her head under water. But today she did it. Over and over again.

As we were leaving class yesterday, I asked the swimming instructor how we could give Tara the confidence to try putting her head in the water. She told me that, sometimes, the tub is a good place to start. Tara was listening to our conversation. She tried it in the tub, quietly. She experimented, closing her eyes and slowly going in more and more.

And today, in class, she did it! She put her whole face, and then her whole head in the water. She beamed—totally beamed—with pride. I was jumping up and down with pride by the side of the pool—an act, which years from now will totally embarrass her. But at least today she was excited and happy. It was a big deal for her.

It amazes me how she overcame her fear.

Quietly. Willing to trust. And then, just taking that critical step forward.

Mallika Chopra

Patience

It was the day after Diwali and I was bracing myself for a family reunion to take place at our home that evening. It was my first in our new house and I wanted to make it a special one for all of us. I was busy coordinating with the florist, caterer, and trying to organise microphones for the ghazal programme when my mother-in-law asked me, for the fifth time, about the menu and who was coming.

'Amma!' I shouted, 'I've told you *four* times already. How am I supposed to get things ready for the evening?' Immediately after the outburst, I felt bad. I realised the pressure of the evening's dinner had really got to me. I ran up to my room and cried for a full half hour.

It was then that I noticed the words, 'Do you love your parents?' on a newspaper lying under my pile of clothes. Suddenly I remembered a story I'd heard years back. I was five then, and sitting in my class with thirty other students. Our teacher Vimlaben had our complete attention as she began the day's story with a question—'Do you love your parents?' How confidently we had all shouted our answer—'Yes!'

Responding to our answers with one of her resplendent smiles, she went on with her story.

An old man was sitting with his forty-five-year-old son. A crow was perched at their window. The father asked his son 'What is that, son?' The son replied, 'It's a crow, father.'

After a few minutes the father asked again, 'What is that, son?' This time, with just a little hint of irritation in his voice, the son retorted, 'I told you just now father, it's a crow.'

A few minutes later the old man asked again, 'What is that my son?' This time the anger was evident in his son's tone as he said, 'It's a crow, a *crow!*'

For the fourth time his father asked, 'What is that, my son?' The son screamed back, 'Why do you keep asking me the same question over and over again? Do you think I have no other work? I just want to read my paper and have my cup of tea in peace!'

The old man got up very quietly and returned with an old tattered notebook in his hand. That notebook was his diary. He opened the page to the day his son had turned three. He requested his son to read the page aloud; he would go to his room and leave his son alone with his tea and newspaper after that, he said.

Impatiently his son began:

Today my little son turned three. We were sitting together on the sofa chatting, when a crow came and sat at our window. He asked me what it was and I told him that it was a crow. With his three-year-old mind, he had difficulty retaining the name of the bird and he asked me about twenty-three times what it was. I answered his question each time, spicing it up with a poem here, some information there, and a few stories about crows as well. Each time he asked me the question, I hugged him; after all who else will he go to with his questions.

Fresh tears streamed down my cheeks as I placed the newspaper aside and rushed to my mother-in-law's room. I hugged her, placed my head on her lap and cried once again, mumbling, 'I am sorry amma, please forgive me.' As parents do, she lovingly raised my head and kissed me on my forehead.

Today both my husband's and my parents are not there anymore. But I am what I am because of those thousands of questions that I must have asked millions of times to them. It was not the answers, but the love and patience behind the answers that makes me the confident, secure person that I am today.

Vrunda Thakkar

The Apple Doesn't Fall Far from the Tree

You tell your child, 'Do not watch so much television, it will teach you nothing and it will spoil your eyes.' Come 9 pm and you are glued to your television set and not a team of wild horses can drag you away. Mommy, are your eyes and brain made of different material?

You tell your child, 'Do not lie.' And the moment the phone rings you instruct her, 'Tell her I'm not here.' Mommy, is lying permitted after you turn eighteen?

You tell your child, 'Respect your elders.' And your child looks at you confused when you give your fifty-year-old cook a verbal dressing down. Ma, is respecting elders subjective?

You tell your child, 'Learn to say thank you.' And you lisp those magic words readily for the smallest thing done by an outsider, but never waste your energy using them for any house members. Mommy, do I have to say thank you only to and in front of outsiders?

You tell your child, 'Why don't you read in your free time?' All your leisure hours are spent discussing the latest who did what and to whom. Mommy, is chatting over the telephone as enlightening as reading?

You tell your child, 'Be generous. Share your toys with your friends.' And you penny-pinch and lie so that neighbours do not develop the bad habit of always coming to your door for whatever they run out of.

You tell your child, 'Learn to let go.' And the child hears you discuss at length the mistake committed by your friend/ husband.

You tell your child, 'Learn to control your temper.' But when you get angry, you shout.

You tell your child, 'Do not hit others.' And you spank, hit or slap your child as punishment.

You tell your child, 'Own up to your mistakes.' But when you make one, you try and rationalise it.

You throw your hands up in exasperation: 'My children never listen to what I say.' But my dear, they are copying you to perfection!

Raksha Bharadia

The Cost of a Threat

I do not remember when the fascination with the sport of gymnastics took root in my daughter, but, somehow, our television set would always be tuned to the sports channel in her spare time. During the Olympics, wild horses could not keep her away from replays of the gymnastics competitions.

Soon she started participating in gymnastics sports events. Being of a petite frame, she did very well in it too, securing a prize in the Indian-Asian meet at Surat. Now she was obsessed with gymnastics and her academic performance started declining. We constantly threatened her: if you don't do well in your exams we will make you discontinue your gymnastics. It seemed to work as she managed to pass even if she did not do too well in some subjects.

She reached the eighth standard and we decided to gradually shift her focus from gymnastics to academics. It was her first term examinations and we commanded her to stop her gymnastics lessons in the mornings and utilise that time to study instead. But she fought tooth and nail to continue her morning sessions and we finally gave in, but with a warning. I said: if you do not pass in all the subjects, no more gymnastics for you, ever.

She came back after writing her mathematics paper, went up to our attic, picked up a can of acid which we kept to recharge batteries, poured some in a glass and drank it.

When the burning sensation in her food pipe became unendurable, she came to us and confessed what she had done. We rushed her to the hospital. Her entire oesophagus canal was burnt.

We have been in and out of hospital for the last three months. I wonder: will she ever be normal, play like other children, be able to do gymnastics... We got her mathematics paper, and yes she had fared badly, scoring nine out of a hundred. Face to face with my child, lying in bed, how small a matter it seemed. One day, about two months after the incident, we happened to be alone. I asked her: did you really want to die? Her eyes swelled with tears. She said: no baba, I just wanted to scare you so that you would never stop me from doing gymnastics. I had no idea what I was getting myself into. I'm sorry, baba.

And then, in the same breath, she asked: baba, will I ever be able to do gymnastics again?

Deep down inside me I felt a gut-wrenching pain. My eyes filled up. I took her in my arms and said: *I'm* sorry, my child, please forgive me. We should never have made that threat.

Today I want to tell all parents out there: never try to use your child's innate love for something—whether it is sports, music or dance—as a weapon to achieve something that is important to *you*. Never threaten your child.

Anonymous

The Photo Session

As the school bus rambled off, my five-year-old daughter breezed in shouting, 'Mama, close your eyes, show me your hand, I have a surprise for you.' I obliged and something soft landed on my palms. Opening my eyes, I found three wilted flowers that she had picked up from our neighbouring street. Beaming her dimpled smile she asked, 'Mama, do you like my surprise?' I hugged her and answered, 'They are lovely.'

It was Children's Day and she had worn a pretty pink dress to school. Sporting two ponytails and wearing matching Bubble Gummers she made a cute picture. Taking out my camera, I told her to pose for me in the balcony and before I could blink she was cat-walking in front of the lens, laughing excitedly. I told her to stand still and focused. As I was about to click, I saw our mashi (a middle-aged lady who comes in daily to save me from doing the monotonous household chores) standing near my daughter, looking expectantly towards me. It took me a minute to understand that she too wanted to be a part of the picture.

Lowering the camera, I said, 'Mashi, please hold the child so that I can take a snap of both of you together.' The smile that lit up her face defied all description. She ventured to hold my daughter close to her and struck a pose. I focused the camera again and what followed came as a rude shock to me. My sweet daughter had lost her dimple and had started to frown. She did not want her pretty picture marred by an ayah, wrapped in a crushed old sari. I tried cajoling a smile out of her and softly told her to hold mashi, but she refused and tried to move away. I tried saving face by telling mashi to hold on to her tightly and desperately clicked.

My camera captured a very disgruntled child straining to get away from her mashi. As I lowered my camera, mashi came to me and said apologetically, 'Didi, I am sorry for troubling you like this but I really wanted to have a photo clicked with Baby (as she affectionately calls my daughter). I've told everyone at home how pretty Baby is and I promised them a picture of hers.' As my face started burning with shame she continued, 'Please do not scold her. She is only a child. Maybe poverty has a figure, shape and style of its own which even a child shies away from.'

Some of my pain poured out in the form of harsh words on my daughter's little head. After the initial storm blew over, I forced myself to cool down and tried explaining the hurt that she must have caused the lady by her uncharitable behaviour. Taking her in my arms, I told her, 'Love, try and remember your Mama's words whenever you come across the poor and needy. It is only by God's grace that you happen to be born into a family where most of your wishes are complied. It takes a second for the Lord to turn the table and you might find yourself in mashi's place. Have love and compassion for the deprived, which will make you into a better human being. I shall frame and give you this picture with mashi. Always keep it with you as a reminder of your Mama's words.'

I was amazed how quickly my five-year-old daughter understood what I was trying to tell her; immediately contrite, she ran up and hugged mashi, apologising for her rude behaviour. With tears in her eyes and a smile on her lips she ordered me to click another snap of hers with mashi. As I focused for the second time I saw a beautiful picture of a child and a woman hugging each other tightly.

Quite a few years have passed since that incident and many mashis have come and gone. The child has remembered my words, growing up to be a compassionate and loving human being. But I have yet to frame that photograph for her, as till date I have not being able to decide which has the greater moral significance of the two snaps clicked on that day, the former or the latter.

Bipasha Roy

The Gift of Life

I opened my wallet and looked at her photograph. *How lovely she looks*, I thought to myself. My life had been a roller coaster until I met her. She meant a lot to me. Well, not 'a lot', she meant *everything* to me!

Suddenly, I heard the door open. A nurse walked out carrying something close to her. She smiled and said, 'Mr Trivedi?' Clearing my throat, I said 'Yes. That would be me.' 'Congratulations, you have a girl. Your wife is alright, but she needs some rest.'

I entered the room behind the nurse, went up to my wife, held her hand and smiled. Her half smile ensured me that she was fine. I had been waiting for this moment for a long time now . . . a moment when I could hold something and enjoy the feeling of possessing it.

She leaned forward and handed my daughter over to me.

I felt her warmth. She was small, delicate, she was simply beautiful, wrapped in this soft white linen that still seemed too rough for her. Till that moment, I used to think she was mine . . . but now I realised it just the opposite. I was hers.

I held her close. The true motive of my life stared at me through those half-opened eyes. I was responsible for her now. I had to protect her, nurture her, love her; not because she was mine but because I was her slave. I knew that I wouldn't, even in my dreams, be able to repay her for what she had given me: happiness, contentment, courage.

My heart now beat within this little being.

I had never held a baby before in my life. I felt awkward. And then I remembered *she* had never been held by anyone in her life. And yet there was no fear in her. If she was not scared to live her first moment then why should I be fearful? She was teaching me things already!

She stopped crying, perhaps because she was in my arms. I thought, 'Will I be able to protect and comfort her always?' The answer was no. She wasn't going to be with me forever. I was taken aback by the thought. A tiny tear rolled down my cheek. I held onto her, promising myself that I wouldn't waste a moment of our time together. I would teach her everything she would want to know. I would prepare her to face the world. I would be there with her forever. I am her father.

I am scared—will I make a good father or a bad one? But I do know this—that I will do my best to make sure that she has a fulfilled life, a happy one. I will make sure that this tiny bundle in my arms will live a better life than I did.

Atul Chaturvedi

Learning

My husband and I had just started a game of Scrabble, when my nine-year-old daughter trotted in and declared that she wanted to join us. Her eleven-year-old friend Trisha was also with her and they formed a team and took the third side on the board. They were doing quite well, scoring around twenty points every round. Mostly their words consisted of four letters with an occasional five-letter word; but I could see that the game had their full concentration. They were stretching their minds and enjoying the challenge.

Now, my husband and I could make words faster and it so happened that my word was set and I had some spare moments before my turn came. With their permission, I looked at the letters my daughter and her friend were holding. They had made the word 'brands' and were extremely proud of their first six-letter word. However, I showed them that, if they put in 'bad' vertically in a way that the 'b' would come in a triple letter score, 'bee' would also form horizontally. The points for their 'b' would then be multiplied six times. Plus, they would save their precious 's' as well.

My suggestion would have been brilliant from the point of winning the game, but is life only about winning and losing?

My child lost her first ever six-letter word in my bid to win. She became less certain about the words she was forming, and began pushing the word tray in my direction so that I would come up with a better scoring word. Towards the end she and her friend simply stopped trying to put words together because I was much faster and better than they were. When we finished the game everyone including me was relieved. Calculating the score was no fun either. Who had scored the most points was irrelevant; we had all somehow lost.

That game of Scrabble made me realise something: we rush to help our children with puzzle pieces, mazes, blocks, forks, spoons, information, maths, words. We think we are trying to be helpful, by either giving them the easy way out or teaching them something more than what they know. But, sometimes, we end up only taking away their right to trial and error, their confidence, their curiosity, their pleasure at discovering something for themselves.

Raksha Bharadia

3

ON TEACHING AND LEARNING

Live as if you were to die tomorrow. Learn as if you were to live forever.
Mohandas Karamchand Gandhi

A Teacher Learns a Lesson

Straight out of training college and a starry eyed twenty-something, I was full of dreams of becoming 'the teacher students would never forget'. I was bubbling with enthusiasm and eager to try out every modern method of teaching that I had been taught in my B.Ed course. I was determined to always be calm, smiling and approachable; and most importantly, to be a picture of confidence before my students. Self-assurance would be my main trait.

Soon, I got a job teaching biology to Class 7 students. Reading out from the prescribed text book, as some teachers do, was not recommended at my training college. I went a step further and asked the class to 'put away' their texts. I would speak, I would write and sketch on the blackboard; they would listen, see, and understand. At least that's what I thought.

One day, as I settled myself at the teacher's desk in the classroom, I looked up to see a timid little girl standing before me. She was so nervous I could see the pulse beating at her temple. I smiled my warmest smile and immediately became the epitome of the understanding, loving, surrogate parent that a teacher is meant to be. Placing her text book before me, she said: 'Miss, please could you mark the portion in the book that you taught yesterday? You're giving us a test tomorrow and I couldn't follow what you taught. I need to study it from the text book.'

My face must have expressed the shock and indignation I felt, for, holding out an envelope, she stammered: 'Daddy said. . . said to ask you.' I unfolded the sheet it contained and read:

Dear Ms Ali,

Please mark the book for the pages on which you are testing the class. Ananya couldn't follow your lecture. And may I please request you to read the lesson with the children in the future. I think class sevens are far too young to retain matter just by listening to a lecture or a discussion.

Ananya stood there, the little mite, biting her lip and waiting for an answer. Forty other students looked back at me waiting to hear my reply. I was suddenly nervous. Also angry, very angry, with this little child and her nosey father who had dared to question my skills as a teacher. So I barked, 'What do you mean you couldn't follow? No one else is complaining and neither would you if you had but paid attention in class. Now get back to your place this instant.'

That evening I related the episode to my father.

'I'm sure you know what you have to do,' he said in his kind, sympathetic manner, not offering me any other advice.

By then my anger had evaporated. Conflicting emotions coursed through me. There was some remorse, some guilt, and lots of self-pity. But I was ashamed of my harsh handling of the little girl. I had not only shown my students how weak I was, I had frightened them, lost their trust, and hurt their feelings.

I did know what to do. I felt defeated. Doubts arose in my mind. Perhaps in my vanity I had been inconsiderate. Perhaps there was a grain of truth in what the girl's father had written. The letter was still in my purse. I took it out and read it again.

I pulled out my letter pad and sat chewing at my pen for a long time. Then I wrote:

Dear Mr Bose

I apologise for scolding Ananya. Having thought through the matter with a cooler head, I realise I may have been too fast for her—and perhaps for other students, too—to follow the lesson. I appreciate your wise suggestion. Even though I will still teach without a text book, I assure you that in future I will make it a point to mark in the text book the portion that I cover in a class. Please reassure Ananya that I am not at all angry with her, though I will tell her the same myself.

The next day I reached the classroom a few minutes early and when Ananya entered I called her over. A worried look on her face, she shuffled towards me.

'Ananya, I'm sorry for getting angry with you yesterday. From today we'll mark the portion being taught in the text book and underline the important definitions and diagrams. Mind you use a pencil, not a pen. And please give this note to your father.'

'Thank you, Ma'am.' She gave me a smile and skipped off to her desk.

The next day Ananya ran up to me and handed me a sealed envelope. 'From Daddy,' she said. Suddenly I was scared again. I turned away from her, not wanting her to see my hands tremble as they tore open the flap. I read:

Dear Ms Ali,

I have not the slightest doubt now that Ananya is in the best of hands. And that is not just because you're a wonderful biology teacher. What makes you the best teacher she can ever have is the humbleness you have shown by your apology and by admitting to your mistake and also your willingness to rectify it. Your students will learn a lot from you and be privileged to have you in their lives.

This happened twenty-six years ago and is a lesson I have always remembered.

Rehana Ali

Anger, Or the Lack of It

I always thought of anger as a natural human emotion: some people were more prone to it, some less, but everyone got angry at some time or the other. Then I got to know Subhash.

Anger was completely alien to Subhash. There were occasions when he expected himself to get angry as well, but no, he would somehow remain calm. Once, he had a problem at the shop that he had rented in the auto parts market. The shop enjoyed a prime location, situated as it was at a corner. Suddenly, the owner approached him, asking for the shop back before the lease period had ended. Subhash did not argue. He vacated the shop and rented another one close by. For a time his sales dropped but soon picked up again. Important as the previous location had been, his quiet manner and genial disposition got him excellent word-of-mouth publicity and attracted customers.

Eventually, Subhash moved on to manufacturing electrical gadgets. He started his own small factory. One night, just as he was falling asleep, he was informed of a fire at the factory. He quickly called the fire brigade and rushed to the factory. Soon the fire was extinguished. He told his scared employees to rest for the night, and that the cause of the fire could be discussed the next day. The fire had caused him significant loss, but Subhash remained cool and calm. The next day he went about enquiring into the mishap. Two employees confessed that the fire could have been put out much earlier had they not been unvigilant and careless. They had been quite lackadaisical in following the emergency procedures. Subhash did not reprimand or lecture them. He merely told them that the fire could have killed them had it not been detected when it had. They realised the enormity of their blunder.

Subhash used to live in a joint family with his two brothers. He and his elder brother were married. When the youngest brother was about to get married they realised that the house was not spacious enough to accommodate another family. There were arguments between his brothers. Quietly, without once being asked to, Subhash moved out. He found a house in the same neighbourhood. After some time, his brothers decided to demolish their house and construct a new one. They told Subhash the new house would have three storeys—one for each brother. He invited them to shift into his house till the new one was built. Upon its completion they all moved back into the new construction. The three brothers now live together happily. One brother's way of life had changed the ways of the others.

Everyone who gets to know Subhash sooner or later comes under his influence. Without any rants or lectures. Since getting to know Subhash I've found myself much more at peace. I find it increasingly easy to control any rising anger. I'm much more cheerful and positive. Subhash showed me that one *can* win wars without a cross word.

Padma Agarwal

Being

My life followed, as most would say, our society's approved sequence. First there was the formal education, followed by a timely marriage, and a career that many women in metros feel or are made to feel incomplete without.

I enjoy writing and so when I finally decided to plunge into some satisfactory work (as opposed to trial and errors), I ended up as a journalist. I worked passionately and loved my work but gave it all up when I was offered a job in the television business as it was considered progression. The cut-throat world of television exhausted me, however, both mentally and physically, and I finally had to distance myself from the medium although people thought it was a bad career move. With nothing else 'to do' I decided to get some of my work as a columnist (that was close to my heart) published in book form. It turned out to be a distasteful experience. As an unknown writer, I was expected to do all the marketing for the book—arrange the eclectic reviewers that would read it, the famous hands that would release it, arrange the crowd that would hopefully buy it, and arrange the journalists to recommend it. They spared me the chairs but I felt more like an event-manager and less of a writer at the end of it all. And

I really didn't care for all the publicity it got me. Something inside broke. Reality sucked.

That was exactly the time it happened. As if synchronised by fate, my first attack, an onslaught of something dangerous and vile, invaded my body. The doctors call it vertigo. One Monday afternoon, three years ago, while carrying my lunch plate from the kitchen, it struck me, as did this fact; a vertigo attack can only be felt, not described. Perhaps like enlightenment. But then enlightenment frees you as much as vertigo binds . . . .

My husband rushed from work with the doctor and the episode ended with a shot in the hip. Very soon I was on the road un-travelled; of brain and body scans, medications and first, second, and third opinions that totalled up to nine specialists. Meniere's Disease, said the one in U.S.A. to our tired faces while we ignored the bottomless pit of our pockets and consumed his conclusion. Then came the truths. One by one; an autoimmune disease, causes deafness, no medical cure, pointless in operating. The End. I had to look elsewhere and so suggestions poured in: pranic healing, psychic surgery, past life regression therapy. I diligently tried them all while my confidence took a beating. There is something about taking health advice from people who haven't experienced chronic disease. They are like an audience whose intellect rises by twenty-five percent the moment the theatre darkens before the movie begins.

I would lie in bed the whole day, and close friends would drop in or gather around me as they did last New Year's Day with dinner plates in their hands. I even missed the damn fireworks outside my window because I could not afford to turn right. A few weeks of this unexpected body breakdown, and I began to panic. Sometime panic, sometime hurt. And where it really hurt was my inability to do something productive work-wise. I was the kind of person who always wanted to have an impressive answer when someone asked me, 'So, what do you do?' The pressure to write my next book from hints in the media, demands by kind readers, and most of all, my own conscience, did not make the inactivity any easier. I was becoming a liability when I was meant to be famous, I thought. Time was passing, was another conditioned thought. Yet, every time I forced myself to write on my laptop an attack was triggered. Soon, I could not sit at all. My attacks only got steadier and stronger and left me feeling debilitated and fearful. Vertigo not only throws you out of balance, it does the same to your life. There is a time to feel old. But it was not now. I was thirty-five. And I needed assistance to go to the bathroom.

Days passed, went into months. I would get attacks as easily as socks slip on feet. And it took days to recover from a full-blown vertigo attack. Through the day I'd wait for my husband to return home from work so we could discuss new moves and methods. Our German Shepherd, Nicholai, who was about eighteen months at this time, and quite finished with the chewing stage, would stay with me the entire time. I would watch his eyes move curiously and the spots above them wriggle funnily in rhythm. His big long nose, wet with health, would heave every now and then to let out a sigh. I would watch his rising and falling stomach, and his alert propped ears, bigger than the wings of some birds. I soon began watching him endlessly, every day, and I can't really say when I started feeling a little better. One day I could prop myself and watch television, or on another, read a page or two. I could even talk on the phone because the ringing in my ears had subsided. In other words, the periods between attacks became longer.

I began to realise that, somehow, this process of observing an animal, a dog, Nicholai, agreed with me. He is a fine dog, I thought, a fine dog that has sensed my condition and is giving me so much compassion by his presence alone. We waited for the same person to return home but in such different ways.

Unlike mine, his wait had an acceptance of his life. He would eat his food, return and wait. He would go for his walk, return and wait. Watching him wait gave me a pleasant feeling. Him, on the wooden floor, beside my bed, waiting. I would curl up as only a prawn can, to face him, so that my senses filled with a behaviour that I wasn't familiar with. When was the last time I had watched a television programme with so much interest? When did anyone I had ever met in life show me what it was to live completely in the moment? This dog could be still for hours, as if on guard, faithful, making me laugh with his failed attempts to catch his tail or trap an annoying fly; making me cry when I longed to play with him. And, above all, he had the ability to become joyful in what I would have called a boring existence. But when you are in a moment for the sake of that moment alone, how can anything be boring?

And that is how simply and gracefully the value of life struck me. I had been greedy and ignorant. Wanting, craving, aspiring ... without realising that all that I wanted, craved and aspired, I already had. I had had it all along. I could once move like the breeze and bend like the weed, but I had chosen to stagnate my thoughts to 'fit in'. How ignorantly I had fallen prey to society's expectations! How could I even compare the joy of playing with my dog to finding a celebrity to release my book? How could I compare the richness in being still and observing creation, to pursuing a stuck-up, embittered television channel for sanctioning a program? Right then, I decided that I would approach life differently. I would become more aware of my present and of my presence.

The minute I got my priorities straight, the right books and messages came my way. I took up ayurveda to follow our ancient path of living a balanced life, and then Rhonda Byrne's The Secret came to me. I began to regularly visualise playing with Nicholai. That became my goal.

Life is strange. I had once wanted to give this dog away, even going so far as to arrange for it. You see, he was a housewarming gift that I couldn't bear because the gift was destroying the new deck chairs, the new carpet, let's say, the new house. I had not learnt to weigh my losses then. Try comparing that to a hearing loss. Now I know. And so, though I lost, I gained too. I gained life's finest lessons from the most unexpected source; I now know that the river of life can suddenly change course. I also know how important it is to become still, still as a curtain that hangs behind a shut window. Still in presence and with integrity where true joys live. I know now that being nothing is the highest order of living, and that it is the rate of our joy that defines the quality of our life . . . .

I can now move freely, twist my neck if needed, write on the computer and yes, play with Nic every single day. I live with my disease, but I have learnt to manage it with joy. There are no more specialists in my life. It's been ten months since my last attack, and that's as old as the last prescription made out to me, which never reached the chemist.

Pallavi Guptaa

Blind Date

This is a story from my struggling days in Mumbai.

After my diploma in acting from the National School of Drama and a stint as a teacher in Lucknow, I came to Bombay to try my luck in Indian movies, which was my ultimate dream. I was thin (could see through a key hole with both my eyes), balding (patchily), and had no money or place to stay—literally. What I had was faith and confidence in my abilities. Soon I started losing that as well—just like my hair. I had exhausted all my friends and relatives' houses for random lunches and dinners, and had borrowed money from every possible and impossible source. It was time to sleep on railway platforms and live on the not-so-fresh air of Bombay. My confidence was at its lowest possible level. No producer was willing to give me work. I would travel in local trains aimlessly. I would take a train from Bandra, go till Churchgate, sit at the station for hours and take a train back to Bandra. For some strange reason I felt the need to be in a crowded place. Being on my own was somehow a constant reminder that I had not achieved anything in life yet.

One day, as I was travelling back to Bandra in that crowded train, there was this man sitting next to me wearing a white kurta pyjama and dark glasses, looking out of the window. He was humming an old Hindi film song. Suddenly, without looking at me, he asked me why I was so restless. I asked him how he knew that I was restless. He said my body language indicated it. After sometime, he said I should wear colourful clothes. I looked at my stained cream coloured T-shirt and kept quiet. Then he said, 'Sometimes a colourful shirt can change your state of mind.' I asked him why he was wearing a white kurta pyjama. He said it was because he was not restless. At Dadar station he got up and walked towards the door of the train, pushing through the crowd. Somebody shouted, 'Get off my foot, can't you see you are standing on it?' Turning around the man said, 'I'm sorry, I didn't see. I am blind,' and disappeared in the crowd.

I looked at my stained T-shirt and wondered at the thought of a blind man talking about colours. Since then, whenever I am feeling low or not in my element or slightly off-colour, I pick up a red shirt and my day changes its colour. Try it . . . it may work for you too . . . .

Anupam Kher

Intelligence and Spiritual Progress

Over the years, I have come to appreciate both the obvious strengths intelligence provides and some of its tremendous dangers. We all know people who become strongly identified with, and attached to their intelligence. It can become a big ego trap, harmful to oneself or others. Intelligence can also be a great blessing, providing invaluable clarity. However, it is important to remember that many other qualities of mind reflect nobility and beauty of character much more than intelligence. Generosity, love, compassion or devotion do not depend on a high IQ.

One of my favourite stories is about a disciple of the Buddha who was considered dull. His brother, another disciple, was an 'arhat', fully enlightened and also very intelligent. The dullard had been inspired by the Buddha's teachings and had been ordained as a monk. He had the sweetest heart, but his mind was slow. Because he was slow, his brother gave him as practice a four-line verse of the Buddha's teachings to memorise.

The boy struggled and struggled to learn one line. Then, as he was trying to learn the second line, he would forget the first. One line was all his mind could retain. This struggle went on and on. His arhat brother finally gave up and said, 'This is hopeless. You had better leave the order of the monks.' The poor boy was totally dejected because his heart was devoted to Buddha.

As he was walking back to his village, the Buddha, aware of what had happened, came and walked by his side. He stroked the poor boy's head and consoled him. Then he gave him a practice exactly suited to him. 'Here's a meditation subject for you,' the Buddha said. 'Take this white handkerchief and stand out in the hot sun and rub it.' That was the whole meditation.

So the boy took the handkerchief, went out in the sun, and began to rub it. Slowly the handkerchief started to become dirty with the sweat from his hand. As that happened, memories awakened in him of previous lifetimes of practice. As he continued to watch the soiled kerchief, a profound dispassion arose and his mind opened. He became fully enlightened. It is said that as he became enlightened, intelligence and all the traditional psychic powers came to him, in addition to a deep understanding of Dharma.

Awakening is for everybody. I think it is fortunate that progress on the path does not depend on the level of one's intelligence. For spiritual practice, there is no partiality regarding intelligence.

Lakshmi Madhusoodanan

Lessons from Children

'I'm out of my wits with you!' my six-year-old niece said to me the other day, frustrated as she was with my stopping her from doing something. I couldn't believe a small girl, just barely waking up to the way the world works—or so I thought—was capable of using such language. I burst out laughing, which she didn't really appreciate, and then kissed and hugged her. I was at once filled with pride at her extremely sharp mind, as well as humbled by it.

Children, we often mistakenly think, are un-grown, empty receptacles waiting for the teachings of the adults around them to fill them up. Over the years, my nieces and nephews have taught me that nothing could be further from the truth. I know now that we learn far more from children then we teach them. The above-mentioned niece, Zuni, and her sibling, eight-year-old Agni, have, since their arrival, been such a source of knowledge about the workings of life for me, that I can't help but think that if we only paid closer attention to the way a child's mind works and let it teach our own embittered, weary, and sad hearts a thing or two, we could all be happier, more fulfilled people.

Now I'm not saying that the motto of life can be found in some simple homily that talks of retaining the 'child within'. What I'm saying is that we mustn't necessarily assume that, as we grow older we also grow up. That we acquire something that those younger than us don't have. When I see my nephew focus with undivided attention on the ball being thrown at him in a game of cricket, I can see that he doesn't need any instructions from me on the virtues of concentration or hard work. He does that quite naturally because he loves the game. When my niece is reading a book and tells me that she wants to read the end after a gap because she wants to save the best for later, I learn so much about the craft of writing. 'The exciting part hasn't yet begun,' she says while reading the beginning chapters, only to squeal with joy a little later, and then close the book so that she can savour the excitement she's feeling for as long as possible, before she reaches the climax. One day she told me, 'Even books have feelings you know,' as she pulled out an old book she hadn't looked at in months and proceeded to read it with the warmth of someone reuniting with a loved one after years. No one likes being neglected, was the clear statement she was making, not even books.

And when I shout at my nephew for being naughty or fighting with his sister, he has forgiven and forgotten all about it a few moments later. He never holds any anger in his heart against me. I marvel at the resilience and strength of a child's heart that is able to do that. And we keep telling ourselves arrogantly that we need to teach values and morals to our children!

Tanuja Chandra

Lessons that Changed my Life

Living with Bapuji at Sevagram, near Wardha, and later at the Dinshaw Mehta Nature Cure Clinic in Pune, Maharashtra, between the ages of twelve and fourteen was a fascinating experience especially since he was my grandfather and I enjoyed the glare of the limelight. I remember him as a strict but loving grandfather who taught me some lessons that made a huge difference in my life.

Anger was a dominant emotion that seethed inside me because of the vicious prejudices I suffered while growing up in South Africa. As if the humiliation of apartheid was not enough, people of colour were often also victims of physical abuse. I was beaten by White and then by African teenagers when I was ten. The pent-up rage resulted in my wanting eye-for-an-eye justice. Fortunately, World War II came to an end and my father Manilal, Gandhiji's second son, decided it was time to visit the family in India.

Bapuji was an astute judge of character and pent up emotions and, at the right time, one day he put his arms around me and in a soft voice said: 'Anger, is like electricity. It is very powerful and useful when used intelligently but extremely deadly and destructive when abused.' The wise thing to do, he said, is to learn to channel anger, just as we channel electricity, and use the energy for the good of humanity. Bapuji said we flare up in anger because we have no control over our mind. We do all sorts of exercises to build a good and strong physical body but neglect the health of our mind. He taught me a very simple exercise. I was asked to sit in a quiet room for a few minutes every day with a flower in front of me. I had to concentrate on the flower for a minute at a time and then shut my eyes and see for how long I could keep the image of the flower in my mind's eye. In the beginning the image vanished the moment I closed my eyes. But when I started doing this exercise every day I found that I could retain that image longer and longer.

Simultaneously, he suggested I write an anger journal so that it became a text book of my emotions. However, he insisted, there would be no point in simply pouring my anger out in the journal. Ideally, the journal should be written with the intention of finding a solution to the problem that caused the anger, and then committing oneself to work out a solution. It was a difficult task, but not impossible. This is a life-long attempt at improving one's disposition and, for the most part, I have been able to use the energy generated by anger for useful and positive purposes.

The second lesson that gave me an insight into his profound philosophy of non-violence was the result of a little three-inch butt of a pencil that I threw away because I wanted a new one. That evening Bapuji made me go out and search for the pencil, and then he told me why it was wrong to throw away something useful. He said when we over-consume and throw away precious resources we commit violence towards nature, and also because of our wasteful habits we over-consume the resources of the world, resulting in economic imbalance so that some people live in affluence while others languish in poverty. That would be violence against humanity. As an adult I began to ponder over this statement and realised how insightful he was. All of us, without exception, commit violence all the time.

Clearly there are two forms of violence—the physical and the passive, or the non-physical. If we do some introspection as religiously as we pray everyday we will discover forms of 'passive' violence that we have no clue about. In a culture of violence where our thoughts, language, habits, behaviour, attitudes, relationships and even religious beliefs are so imbued with violence, there are so many hurtful things that we do every day, consciously and unconsciously, that we would be amazed at ourselves. The simple yardstick that Bapuji used is to ask one's conscience: 'Is the action I contemplate selfishly motivated? Will it hurt people? Will it improve the lives of the masses?' Ultimately, it is the over-whelming commission of passive violence that generates anger in the victim who then resorts to physical violence to get justice. So, the logical conclusion is that 'passive' violence becomes the fuel that ignites 'physical' violence committed by the disaffected and the destitute to vent their anger and frustration. This is why Bapuji said: 'We must become the change we wish to see in the world.'

Bapuji's non-violence, I concluded, is not negative at all, because to practice non-violence or satyagraha one has to allow love, respect, understanding, compassion, acceptance and appreciation, all positive attitudes and emotions, to supersede, whereas in the existing culture of violence we are dominated by hate, prejudice, discrimination, oppression, and the myriad negative attitudes and emotions that are self-destructive like cancer. No wonder civilisation today is faced with a mammoth crisis of conscience.

Arun Gandhi

Life is Baeutiful

Do you remember the name of your kindergarten teacher?
I do, mine. Her name was Mrs White. And I remember
thinking she must be an older relation of Snow White, because
she had the same bright blue eyes, short dark hair, red lips
and fair skin.

I don't remember much about what we learned in her class,
but my mother once told me that we used to write a lot. And
I would bring back what I wrote and she would look at it and
see there were so many mistakes. But no corrections marked
in red. And always a star. Sometimes even a Good! scrawled
on the side, which would make my heart soar with happiness.
But it worried my mother, so one day, when she went in to
meet Mrs White for one of those Parent-Teacher meetings, she
asked her why she never corrected my mistakes. Why she
never red-pencilled in the right spellings of words or pointed
out grammatical errors.

And my mother says Mrs White said: The children are just
beginning to get excited about using words, about forming
sentences. I don't want to dampen that enthusiasm with red
ink. Spelling and grammar can wait. The wonder of words
won't . . . . Maybe she didn't say it exactly like that. It was a

long time ago, and what my mother told me was the gist of what she could remember. The rest I added in. Because I grew up learning to use words with loving confidence exactly the way Mrs White intended us to.

It occurs to me that if Mrs White had used her red pen more precisely I probably wouldn't be telling you about this now. Which is kind of obvious but also kind of not. I look back now and think she must have been a rather extraordinary teacher—to exercise such red-pen-restraint. To allow the joy, wonder and excitement of expression to flower—however faultily—like that. Because to bloom is better than not to bloom. And a bud once nipped never opens. May we all be so kind . . . .

I used to misspell beautiful a lot. Never could quite remember that the e went before the a. It exasperated my teacher in high school no end. If I was going to employ the word with such lavishness, she figured the least I could do was spell it right. Eventually the e's and a's settled into their right places of their own accord. I'm glad I didn't worry too much about it though. Pretty is easier to spell but it doesn't hold as much as you mean sometimes. And thanks to Mrs White, I had no qualms about writing what I meant even if I couldn't quite spell it out. Because Life isn't Pretty. It's Baeutiful.

Pavithra Mehta

My Grandfather's Legacy

I always looked up to my grandfather. When I was younger I would help him in little ways, which was quite a task since he dedicated his life to helping others. My grandfather believed that small is beautiful, and served people in little ways: mending a mattress, getting someone their day's milk, caring for the sick. He always insisted that I join his efforts. Irritation or anger would usually be my first reaction to his request. I could not understand why he would want to spend so much time with others. But then I would watch him in action and feel guilty that he was working so hard at such an old age.

Preparing afternoon tiffins for the sick was something he did quite often. When he would go on his delivery run, I would decline to help, making some excuse or the other. One of the sick people he assisted was a woman who suffered from cancer. She eventually passed away, six months after which my grandfather was diagnosed with cancer. My family told me he was sick but I did not understand the extent of it. In fact nothing between my grandfather and me really changed, and he never let on how ill he was. Then one day, after I had taken an exam, my mom came to school, crying and insisting that I visit my grandfather, who had been admitted to hospital. I rode my bike to the civil hospital, unprepared for the condition that I would find him in. Surrounded by all the people that loved him, I had to part through the crowd to find my grandfather. When I did, I could not bear what I saw. He had grown so frail. Cervical cancer had robbed me of my beloved grandfather. I started crying. When my grandmother asked him if he knew who I was, he called me by another name. I was shattered. He passed away soon after.

I was angry and illogically blamed the woman who had cancer for my grandfather's illness and death. The idea of helping other people seemed futile. In the meanwhile, some of my good friends had been working with a local NGO and encouraged me to come with them. I finally conceded and accompanied them one day. The experience inspired me and I decided to start working with the organisation. For one of my first assignments, I had to go to the civil hospital to help a boy from the slums that had been infected with cancer. While in the hospital, I was overwhelmed by a feeling to visit my grandfather's old room. I never did. I stayed with the young boy, helped him through his check-up and getting his medicines. I was able to help the boy in some little way, and knowing that filled me with great joy. Suddenly I understood what my grandfather had been doing his whole life. Today I work as computer teacher at the same organisation and have found my own ways to step in my grandfather's very big shoes.

Vijay Jadav

My Lucky Charm

I found my first quiz book in a used-book store when I was twelve, and it soon became a passion. So, on entering the sixth standard in school, when we were offered a choice of Quiz and Public Speaking as an optional extracurricular activity, I jumped at it. It was then that I met Mr Errol O'Brien, a retired tea taster, and now a rare male teacher in Ballygunge Shiksha Sadan, an all-girls school in Kolkata.

With Mr Brien, it was never about memorising the facts in quiz books. Instead, it was about opening our senses and becoming aware of the world around us. Once I had memorised a list of famous books and their authors; as I showed off to the others my two-hundred-strong list of weighty books and even weightier names, a simple question from Mr Brien stumped me. 'But my girl, have you actually read these books?' He made us delve deeper, look beyond the surface.

Once, he took us on a tour of Kolkata. Though we visited the usual landmarks like the Victoria Memorial and the Raj Bhavan, he also showed us a side of the city most tourist guidebooks miss. Hidden behind the overgrown shrubbery and crumbling ruins of St. John's Church, we discovered the grave of Job Charnock, the founder of Kolkata. He told us his story. Till then, Charnock had been just a name for us. That day I saw a different side to my city, one which no book would ever have been able to teach me.

Initially we used to fare poorly in the quiz contests we participated in, but step-by-step we improved. From the new kids on the block and the also-featured, we became actual contenders. As the trophies started coming in, the criticisms that had come our way for taking off all that time from our academics started dying down. But more than the laurels, we earned respect. We earned the right to hold our heads up high. When we went out to other schools to take part in quizzes, we hardly ever had a cheering squad accompanying us. I remember the first time we realised that something in the air had changed. We were on the verge of winning a major quiz, and the audience, none of them our schoolmates, erupted with cries of 'BSS . . . BSS . . . BSS' every time we answered. More than the trophy we won, I cherish the warmth of all the people who cheered on these unknown girls that day.

Mr Brien was there with us throughout. Modest as he is, he'd always claim that, in spite of all that goes on backstage, it is the players who take the field, and not the coach, who carry the day. Little did he know that we made him part of the entire proceedings by scribbling his initials, EOB, on our rough sheets at every quiz. EOB was our lucky mascot.

Mr Brien didn't just teach us about quizzing or public speaking. That might have been his initial job description, but with time the roles of counsellor, friend, confidant, father figure and role model were all added to the ever-expanding list. I was in the eighth standard when we qualified for the finals of the All Asia Bournvita Quiz Contest. The televised episodes were to be shot in Sri Lanka. This was to be my first overseas trip and it added to the excitement of representing my school at the national level. Less than a week before our departure, I fell sick. I was throwing up everything that went down my throat. I felt physically weak and, worse, mentally drained. All my confidence vanished. I was scared of travelling so far away from home without my parents. I was petrified of making a fool of myself in the contest and letting my team down.

I went over to Mr Brien's place for one last session before we left. Unable to take it any longer, I blurted out all my insecurities to him. He looked at me for a while and then, without saying a word, went into his bedroom. After a while he returned with a really old magazine in his hand. 'My girl, this is a St. Xavier's Collegiate School magazine from 1956. There's a certain article in here I want you to read,' he said. It was an article on the Annual Inter-Jesuit Elocution Competition. It had been won that year by a sixteen-year old who had mesmerised the audience with an inimitable rendition of Edgar Allan Poe's *The Tell Tale Heart*. There was also a sepia-toned photograph of the boy along with the article. The caption below it read, 'Errol O'Brien with his trophy'.

'That article won't tell you what I had to overcome to win that competition,' he said, going on to explain that a couple of days before the competition, an unfortunate accident had knocked out two front teeth. More than the pain, he was overwhelmed by the fear of becoming the laughing stock of the school by messing up the piece he was going to recite. 'I was literally in tears, terrified that I would stutter and ruin my piece. But if I had simply given up that day, I wouldn't have been able to go back to my alma mater every year to judge this very same competition.'

That day I learnt something precious which has kept me going ever since. It's alright to have moments of self-doubt and despair. There are times when the going gets too tough and giving up seems so much an easier option. But what's important is how we deal with these feelings that get us down. We cannot deal with our inner demons by denying their existence, but by acknowledging them and their power to hurt us. Beyond intangible fear lies the reality of all that is precious enough to fight for.

There was just one thing left for me to say. 'I'll give it my best shot, Sir.'

We didn't come back with the trophy that year. But I know that I did keep my word.

About a month ago, I went back to school to take part in an alumni quiz. Mr Brien was there as well; he never misses a good quiz. Sitting in the audience, he answered a particularly difficult question and won himself a bottle of wine. All his students, past and present, broke into applause. According to the quizmaster, 'his fans are here to cheer him on'. Yes, we were there to cheer him on. He was there to do the same for us when nobody else was betting their money on the underdogs, not even the underdogs themselves. But sometimes faith and hard work make all the difference. That and a lucky charm called EOB.

Preyoshi Ganguly

One Man's Family

When the tsunami came, I was barely touched. I worked for a large software company in Bangalore, and the only disaster I knew of, was not meeting my quarterly revenue targets. Yet, life makes choices for you sometimes. One day, when I was discussing the tsunami with a colleague, he said, 'But what can we do?' I felt thunderstruck. I was twenty-five, fit, healthy, employed, with an MBA to boot. And yet I did not seem to have an answer to this simple question: 'What can I do?'

Three days later, I reached Car Nicobar, one of the southernmost islands in the Andaman and Nicobar archipelago, and the worst hit by the tsunami. A quarter of the island's population, nearly five thousand people, had been wiped out by the tsunami. The rest had fled into the jungles in the interior of the island. I volunteered to work with the Army and paramilitary troops scouting trails in the jungle, taking count of the survivors, and delivering relief supplies. After ten days of effort, fatigue began to hit me, as did doubt. In the nights, when we trekked under the clear, tropical sky, I often wondered if I knew what I was doing. I was absent without leave from work, and I wondered if I would still have a job when I got back to Bangalore.

And then I met Philip. That day, I was leading a group of men from a village which had been totally cut off from the rest of the island by the tsunami. An army officer, Lt Col Bisht, and I, had earlier managed to reach the village by helicopter and bring in essential supplies. But the rations would soon run out and we needed to connect the village to the outside world fast. I had organised a group of men from the village to hack a trail through the jungle to the nearest connected village. Initially there were two hundred of them, but after two hours, when I looked back and took count, there were only ten. Most had returned to their settlements. I felt angry because we still had miles of jungle to cut through. When the remainder of the group of ten started turning back, I stopped them. I tried to persuade them to the best of my abilities. I told them this trail was for the future of the village, for every one of their children who needed to go to school in the neighbouring village, as their own school had been destroyed by the tsunami. This trail would become a road that was their own. But they were tired and weak from weeks of near starvation, and I wasn't sure if I was getting through to them.

Not seeing any immediate response, I said angrily that I would hack the trail myself if needed and asked if there was even one who would join me. A short young man stepped up and said he would. Together, we left the group and started hacking the trees and vines. Minutes later, to my great surprise, I noticed that one after another, all the men in the group walked up and joined us. I was amazed. I wanted to know who this young man was, for it was certainly he that was the prime mover—the catalyst—for the change. I asked him about himself. His name was Philip. He was twenty-five, the same age as me. But there the similarity ended. He had lost his wife and child two weeks previously in the tsunami. But this trail, he said, was necessary to get medicine for the ailing children of the village. No one must die, he said.

'No one must die.' I suddenly felt as if my work had found meaning. Suddenly, sales targets and software did not matter as much. As I watched Philip hack through the foliage, I thought about him. This brave man, despite such tremendous personal tragedy, had stepped up because he considered the village his family. He wasn't just cutting a trail, I felt; he was showing me the way.

Raja Karthikeya

Learning from Experience

1. I will begin with the importance of learning from experience. It is less important, I believe, where you start. It is more important how and what you learn. If the quality of the learning is high, the development gradient is steep, and, given time, you can find yourself in a previously unattainable place. Learning from experience, however, can be complicated. It can be much more difficult to learn from success than from failure. If we fail, we think carefully about the precise cause. Success can indiscriminately reinforce all our prior actions.

2. A second theme concerns the power of chance events. As I think across a wide variety of settings in my life, I am struck by the incredible role played by the interplay of chance events with intentional choices. While the turning points themselves are indeed often fortuitous, how we respond to them is anything but so. It is this very quality of how we respond systematically to chance events that is crucial.

3. Of course, the mindset one works with is also quite critical. As a recent work by the psychologist, Carol Dweck, has shown, it matters greatly whether one believes in ability as inherent or that it can be developed. Put simply, the former view, a fixed mindset, creates a tendency to avoid challenges,

to ignore useful negative feedback and leads such people to plateau early and not achieve their full potential. The latter view, a growth mindset, leads to a tendency to embrace challenges, to learn from criticism and such people reach ever higher levels of achievement (Krakovsky, 2007: page 48).

4. The fourth theme is a cornerstone of the Indian spiritual tradition: self-knowledge. Indeed, the highest form of knowledge, it is said, is self-knowledge. I believe this greater awareness and knowledge of oneself is what ultimately helps develop a more grounded belief in oneself, courage, determination, and, above all, humility, all qualities which enable one to wear one's success with dignity and grace.

Based on my life experiences, I can assert that it is this belief in learning from experience, a growth mindset, the power of chance events, and self-reflection that have helped me grow to the present.

Back in the 1960s, the odds of my being in front of you today would have been zero. Yet here I stand before you! With every successive step, the odds kept changing in my favour, and it is these life lessons that made all the difference.

My young friends, I would like to end with some words of advice. Do you believe that your future is pre-ordained, and is already set? Or, do you believe that your future is yet to be written and that it will depend upon the sometimes fortuitous events?

Do you believe that these events can provide turning points to which you will respond with your energy and enthusiasm? Do you believe that you will learn from these events and that you will reflect on your setbacks? Do you believe that you will examine your successes with even greater care?

I hope you believe that the future will be shaped by several turning points with great learning opportunities. In fact, this is the path I have walked to much advantage.

A final word: when, one day, you have made your mark on the world, remember that, in the ultimate analysis, we are all mere temporary custodians of the wealth we generate, whether it be financial, intellectual, or emotional. The best use of all your wealth is to share it with those less fortunate.

I believe that we have all at some time eaten the fruit from trees that we did not plant. In the fullness of time, when it is our turn to give, it behooves us in turn to plant gardens that we may never eat the fruit of, which will largely benefit generations to come. I believe this is our sacred responsibility, one that I hope you will shoulder in time.

N.R. Narayan Murthy
Pre-commencement lecture at the New York University
Stern School of Business

Sonu

I lay sprawled on the rubble, peering into a crevice in the concrete in front of me. She was definitely inside. The thought made me miserable. It was 30 January 2001, three days after the worst earthquake to ever hit India, and I was in Bhuj, assisting in the rescue work. The rest of the rescue team, unlike me, who was a college student, were professionals and were cutting their way through layers of concrete to reach the victim who lay trapped under tons of concrete. We'd heard faint noises from this building and had rushed here, but the operation was proving to be tough. I tried to discern the position of the victim, through the darkness of the crevice, so that she wasn't harmed by the drilling. As the noise of the rescue team's hydraulic drill reached a crescendo, there was a faint scream from inside. I realised to my horror that lying under all the rubble was a girl, a little girl, maybe three or four years old.

I found out from a neighbour that her name was Sonu. I wasn't sure what to do, but I wanted to calm her down. She had to stay still so that the concrete would not collapse on her. I told Sonu not to worry, that her parents were waiting for her outside (in fact they had died, along with her brother, in the quake). She screamed again at the noise of the drill. I told her it was a machine, just like her toy train. She relaxed a bit. I told her to stay still so that we could get her out fast, to her parents, and they could all then go the mela which had come to town. She mumbled yes weakly. I told her I'd get her a Pepsi if she stayed still. Then to my surprise, she said, 'I want a Frooti!' And then, 'I want *two* Frootis.'

Amidst the dust, the noise, and the merciless heat of the Kutch, I couldn't help smiling. This little girl had lain buried for three days in total darkness, trapped under a chair that had protected her from the collapsed ceiling. She had been hungry, afraid, and helpless for three days, and yet she had not given up on her zest for life.

Minutes later, as the crevice became an opening, my colleague Eric and I reached in and pulled Sonu from under the chair in one swift move before the concrete caved in. As Sonu was carried away to an ambulance, the rescue crew, soldiers and the crowd standing around, who had worked till then in grim silence unearthing bodies and remains of homes, suddenly started clapping. It was the first sound of joy I heard in Bhuj that winter.

Raja Karthikeya

The Alchemy of Nature

To see a world in a grain of sand
And a heaven in a wild flower,
Hold infinity in the palm of your hand
And eternity in an hour

William Blake

We instinctively turn to outdoor activities and nature as a way of relaxing and enhancing our well-being. Nature soothes and nurtures. Nature fulfils and motivates. Nature whispers and commands.

Are you listening?

When I do, it leaves me in complete awe.

We have a hibiscus plant in our garden. Every fortnight a flower blooms on it—big, bright and tender. Through the day it smiles with the sun and dances with the wind, but as evening approaches, it starts wilting. The morning after, it withers completely and by evening it falls and becomes one with the earth again. The flower comes to life only for a day, yet it does so in full splendour. What if we too lived our life, however short, to its fullest?

We went to a rocky beach and saw the spread of the majestic ocean and the rocks alongside, carved, sculpted and shaped by the water. Water is so soft, rock so hard, yet, as the water flows over it every day, for years, the rock gives in. It takes the shape that the water commands. Our problems are so colossal and we are so small, yet if we persist . . .

We saw small bits of grass peeping through the small cracks in a concrete pavement. It left us thinking: however impossible things may look, there is always an opening . . .

We saw a tree bare of all leaves in the cold winter months. We thought its chapter was over. But three months passed, spring set in and the tree was back to its green majesty once again, full of leaves, flowers, birds and life. What if we too had the conviction that, however difficult things are right now, it will not remain so for ever. Remember, this too shall pass.

We saw an army of ants lugging a fly which was at least ten times the ant's size. The ants organised themselves around the fly, lifted it on their frail feelers and carried it to quite a distance. Their teamwork and perseverance were impressive. What if we too are consistent, organised, focused...

Spider webs are delicate, yet very strong. A rainbow colours the entire sky. Oysters take in a grain of sand and open up with a pearl. Innumerable stars shine across the infinite sky. Clouds take new shapes with every passing moment. The wind makes the trees dance with unhindered passion. Water, without a hint of ego, changes its form according to the dictates of the sun and the wind. When we see a caterpillar turn into a butterfly, a flower turn into a fruit, we experience the alchemy of nature . . . we touch it and become gold ourselves.

Raksha Bharadia

The Biker

I have a Royal Enfield Thunderbird but this note isn't about either of us

it's about a guy in my office complex who drives an Enticer to work every day

his Enticer is fitted with extra wheels on the side, like a child's cycle

no, he's not a wimp

he's probably the bravest man I've seen

you see, the thing is that this guy doesn't walk

he crawls

his legs are twisted and bent under him, like a tortoise coil made out of skin and sinew

like the sweet god of creation changed his mind halfway only halfway

so every day, he inches forward like a gravel swimmer, slowly, painfully

and proudly

I feel like rooting for him, clapping like a wound-up toy monkey

but to do so would be to acknowledge what he's fiercely forgetting every minute of his life

so I stay quiet, avert my gaze till I hear the roar of the
motorcycle
only then do I turn to see him riding away
I don't even know his name
but I know that I'm five feet eight inches tall and that he
towers over me.

Ram Cobain

The Little Girl

It was only when the mild drizzle had graduated to swollen drops falling noisily on the windowsill next to my workstation that I noticed the change in weather. My tired eyes shifted from the computer screen to the scene outside. It was a rather heavy downpour, and I could see the sky turning darker. The wind hissed with pleasure or displeasure, I cannot say, since my mind was occupied with the thought of the extra hour or two that Delhi's traffic would snatch from my day as an aftermath of the showers. I walked to the vending machine to satisfy my urge for a cup of steaming coffee but I could not bear to consume the repulsive liquid disguised as coffee ejected from the vending machine; it seemed to be the last straw in an already bad day.

I returned to my workstation but this time chose to stand by the window that overlooked the construction site of a hotel. The half constructed building was surrounded by a rather sizeable muddy area; on a small patch of this stood a few huts of labourers who were working there. I wondered if the huts were protecting the labourers; would they be allowed a peaceful sleep after a day of hard work. My attention shifted . . . perched in front of one of the small huts, I saw a little girl. Long unkempt hair, and dressed in tattered clothes, she swung from a rope tied in the entrance of the hut, perhaps her home. She did not look older than ten years. As I was speculating her age, I saw her gleefully stretch out her legs with an outward swing, allowing the rain to drench her. And with that act, she dropped her head back and laughed out loud. For the next few minutes, she sang and clapped and swung higher, oblivious of the risk of falling and hurting herself. I peered harder and saw a sparkle in her eyes that I hadn't seen in many years. Her face shone with contentment, contentment that had long eluded me. She did not seem bothered about the day ahead or the sleepless night that she might have to spend. She seemed unaffected by the possibility of a life that she might have to suffer in misery.

In that moment, I suddenly felt inadequate in my approach and limited in my thinking. Perhaps I had simply stopped looking at the right places for peace and contentment. Perhaps I chose not to look at everyday blessings as I became totally consumed with my greater needs. When last had I felt peace that I had my loved ones by my side? Did I thank god today for the rains that I had loved once? Would I find contentment in jumping in a puddle or feeling raindrops on my fingers? I closed my eyes amazed at how much I had already missed.

The little girl was still laughing and singing while I silently thanked her with all my heart.

Shilpa Malhotra

The Walk that Changed His Life

Milind Gupta was a very busy man with many responsibilities. He had a business to run. He was the eldest son and his parents were too old to take charge of the complicated affairs of the joint family, so he had to handle every little thing. His sister's daughter's engagement, a job for his uncle's son, tension between his younger brother's wife and her daughter-in-law—all of this landed on his plate.

Milind never complained, but one day in the middle of a board meeting, he felt his head spin. He collapsed. He had to be taken to hospital, but he was more worried about the big, business deal they had lost. He told his doctor he had to be back on his feet as soon as possible.

Milind's doctor was a wise man who had seen many patients like him—people so stressed out by their lives that they didn't have the time to see how stressed they were. When Milind finished talking about his business problems and how important it was to get back to work, the doctor gently drew him out about his family life. For the first time in many years, Milind spoke of his difficulties, of how he never got any rest, of how tired he was of sorting out everyone's finances, marriages, children's problems.

'If you don't find a way to rest,' the doctor told Milind, 'you will die. I want you to do something. Every evening, no matter what you do, take a walk. Now this is important. You need to walk for your health, but you are a heart patient and you mustn't overdo it. So from your house, I want you to walk to the temple down the road. Sit in the temple for ten minutes. This is just to catch your breath and give your heart a rest. Then walk back home. But you have to do this at the same time every day.'

Milind promised his doctor he would do this, but he was already feeling tense at the thought of finding the time. The first day, he almost forgot, but his doctor had foreseen this and called his secretary, who reminded him to go.

All the way to the temple, Milind could think of nothing but the meeting he was missing because of this walk. He set his cell phone alarm for ten minutes exactly, annoyed at the noise of the temple bells around him. His mind was on the tasks he would do when he got back, and the talk he had to have with his nephew about his career options.

Neither the walk nor the temple had done anything for him, Milind thought as he walked out, the doctor was a fool.

As he reached the gate, Milind saw a much older man lose his footing on the stairs and slip. The man was frail, his face lined, but his clothes were neat and spotless. Milind hesitated, then went over to help the man up. He found his walking stick and handed it to him.

'Thank you, beta,' the older man said. He was still shaky from his fall. 'I hate to trouble you,' he continued, 'but would you help me, just until the shrine?' A thousand thoughts flashed through Milind's mind. He would be late. His work would pile up. But he found himself saying yes.

The man made his way slowly to the temple, leaning on Milind. When they reached, he thanked Milind again. 'My son used to do this for me,' he said. 'But he died several years ago, in a car accident.' Milind said with automatic politeness, 'You must miss him a lot.'

The older man looked at him for a long moment. 'You look like a busy man yourself, so maybe you will understand. I never knew my son, not well. I was always too busy with work, with managing the family, all of that. So all his life, we never sat down and talked. This was the only time I took off for myself, and that was because my wife insisted. He would come on his own from work every day to escort me in, but my mind was always on my own work. We never talked much when he was alive. I would rush in, sit here for ten minutes, plan the rest of my working evening, and leave—sometimes I didn't even notice he was there.'

Milind found himself saying, 'I am so sorry.'

The older man smiled. 'Don't be, beta. Every day, I come here and I try to find one person to talk to who looks as though he might need to hear this story. I wish I had found that person before my son died. But since I can't do it for myself, I do it for other people.'

A suspicion crossed Milind's mind. 'Did you slip on purpose?' he asked. The older man smiled. 'Sometimes we have to stumble and fall so that others will see the obstacles in their path and avoid them,' was all he said.

As he walked back, his tiredness briefly lifted, Milind knew that he had found something precious in this brief encounter with a stranger. Everything that had seemed so important and crucial in his life had kept him from seeing what was truly significant. He knew his life would be different from now on, and he silently blessed the doctor who had made him take the walk that changed his life.

Meetu Chatterjee

The Welcome Silence

I was a non-confrontational person; I believed in taking the middle path, never fighting back in an argument, never raising my voice. Unless it was absolutely necessary, I didn't voice an opinion. For all I knew, I didn't have much of an opinion on anything. You could say I was that easy-going person who lives and loves quite easily, happily.

I guess I was brought up that way. Being the only daughter of a widowed mother and, not exactly dependent on, but unable to refuse people's hand-me-downs, books, clothes, money—had kept me humble. We never made a fuss and mother was always thankful to these people. She always made it a point to return these favours in kind when she made a coconut cake or homemade wine. They in turn never forgot us in the impulses of generosity that occasionally possessed them.

So, as I was saying, I was an extremely non-confrontational person, and if at all I had to call a spade a spade, I would do so hesitantly, politely.

When I finished college, I got a job in the firm my father had worked in. The manager of the firm was an old family acquaintance, and he had kept me in mind for the job when my father died. So I didn't even have to fight through an interview process or tough competition.

At work, I maintained a cordial, balanced relationship with everyone. I got along with everyone: I shared lipstick tips with the 'fashionables' even though I didn't wear much make-up, asked for recipes from the senior women, and exchanged guarded pleasantries with the managers.

All in all, I was the most peaceful person one could meet, so it came to me as a surprise when, one day, I found in me strength that I never thought I had. I had just walked into the house after work, when my mother, in a panicked state, told me that my father's brother—an uncle I had never met—had shown up to claim his share of our house, the only asset we owned. Apparently he had lost a lot of land and property in his village because of a landslide.

Shocked, I asked my mother, 'Does he have a right to the house?'

'No, the house is ours. I inherited it from your father after he died. It will go to you eventually.'

'Then how does he come into the picture?' I asked.

'Because there was no will made, he says that, as your father's brother, he has claim to half the property. He was also talking about having lent some money to your father when the house was bought twenty-seven years ago.'

My head reeled with the thought of the possible years we were likely to spend in courts.

'Did daddy mention how much money he had borrowed?'

'No, he never mentioned borrowing money, and that makes me think that this man is lying,' my mother said. I could see beads of sweat rolling down the side of her face.

'What are we to do?' she said finally. 'He has gone to get other men. I heard him talking on the phone. We have to call the neighbours.'

Now if you, like me, have ever taken favours, and not once but many times, you will know that it is not an easy existence.

And though kind people do not ask for anything in exchange, they certainly don't expect you to depend on them or disturb them for everything. Also, I suddenly found that I didn't *want* to take any more favours. I wanted to handle this on my own.

'Let's see what we can do,' I finally told my mother, releasing a breath.

'Let's call Sheik Uncle or Nirupama Aunty,' urged my distraught mother.

'No, we have to handle this,' I said. 'How many times, ma, do you think we should call in people to help us?'

The sound of the doorbell cut right through our hearts like a knife. I looked through the peephole, and saw several men looming on the other side of the door. I could sense their force. My mind was racing, my throat dry. If I had to do something, it was now. I didn't have the money, even though I was earning, to go to courts or pay lawyers; nor did I have the time, what with my job, housework and taking care of my arthritic mother. I drew in a breath and opened the door.

The men were looking at me with hired menace.

'Come inside uncle,' I said to the person I assumed was my relative. He looked like my father, but a cynical, weather-beaten, version.

'Would you like to sit while we wait?'

'Wait? Wait for what?'

'The police, of course,' I said, 'they are on their way. I just telephoned them and, you know, they are also going to your village to help the other victims of the landslide.' My heart beat against my chest like a window in a cyclone.

My uncle looked at me, and his face fell. 'I see,' he said finally.

I was trying to suppress the sense of triumph that had started to rise in my guts. I wondered quietly if the battle was over as yet. The other men, three of them, looked at my uncle, waiting for his next order.

'I think then, we need to go,' said my uncle in a softer tone. 'I will need to tell the police what happened.' He forced a chuckle: 'You know how the police are...' he said, half-addressing the hired men who nodded and left with him.

I quickly bolted the door, *my* door, and went back inside to find my mother praying, her head bowed before the altar. I silently embraced her. The silence was louder than any noise I have heard before and it was the silence of a peace that I think you witness just sometimes in life when you manage to stand up for yourself and your loved ones.

Rochelle Potkar

With Dignity

She was sweeping the room with a concentration that surprised me.

I had met her earlier that day and we had enjoyed some conversation. One of the many staffers in the Indian Airlines Sales office, she seemed to be a friendly sort and smiled each time our eyes met.

Then, as I sat about waiting for my turn to speak at a workshop I was conducting, she came up to chat.

She asked questions about me, we traded facts about our respective children, and she told me her daughter, all of nineteen, was studying to be a dentist. 'She's very smart, my daughter is,' she added, with the pride of a mother who knows she has brought up her child right.

She wanted to know of avenues for growth, how the girl could progress in life, she had opinions on the status of the country, on the political mess we were in; her statements were balanced and well articulated; she had obviously given the subjects much thought.

Then, later in the afternoon, I saw her walking past with a broom, and a little later when I went back out of the hall again, to wait out the next lecture, I saw her sweeping the room. She worked slowly and deliberately, making sure no dust remained hidden under the table or chairs.

I thought she was probably allergic, and had decided to clean her room herself.

She looked up at me and smiled.

'How far have you studied?' she asked me. I told her. She smiled appreciatively. 'I tell my daughter that studies are a wealth that no one can take away,' she remarked. 'You can wear your wealth on your person as gold, or stash it away as money, it is always in danger of being robbed, but education is within you, it will always help you in times of need more than money or jewellery can.'

'Look at me,' she continued. 'I lost out because I did not have enough education.'

I looked at her, and saw nothing to betray her uneducated status. Her sari uniform was neatly pinned to her shoulder and as well draped as any of the others in the office; her hair, partly grey and in need of touching up, was nonetheless pinned to her head in a close bun. Her eyes were bright and her smile ready.

She saw me looking at her, taking in the details. 'I came here for a job, and they said, "you are only tenth pass", and they put this broom into my hand.... That's all I have been doing since,' she said.

I wondered how she could be so sanguine about it all. Her knowledge was formidable, her conversational skills were good, she was affable and spoke good, grammatically correct English. The loophole she fell through was one of formal education; to me she was more 'educated' than some of my colleagues in the MA class had been.

I wondered too, if her daughter worried about her job and its reflection on her own status among her peers. This lady was definitely not of the same ilk as the others who were helpers there; though they wore uniforms, there was a distinct difference in their approach to their work, in their view of life. But to the outside world, they were all of one station.

I wondered too, if she had been forced to take up this job to educate her daughter; was she the one bearing the financial burden of a professional education in the process of ensuring that her daughter never had to pick up or wield a broom, at least not in public. It was all very mystifying; she did not seem to belong to a broom-wielding background; was there no way an organisation could change its employment rules to make concessions where they were really needed?

As the day ended, she got ready to leave. She emerged from the changing room in a salwar kurta, which was pretty and unusual. I remarked on it, she told me where she had bought it ... it was a shop known for its elegant readymades.

She held her hand out in goodbye and as I took it, she leaned forward and kissed me on the forehead.

'It is so nice to meet a new friend,' she said smiling warmly.

She then picked up her bag, and prepared to leave. 'I will be back only on Monday, when you won't be here,' she said, 'but I will tell my daughter I met you. She reads your paper. In fact we are gold card DNA holders.'

I felt my throat constrict. I had been giving lessons all through the three days on self-confidence, but had learnt a lesson myself. About the dignity of labour, of never being ashamed of a job as long as it was well done.

As I watched her retreating back, I took my imaginary hat off to her.

Sathya Saran

The Sharing of Wealth

I belong to a prominent business family and am well aware of the tussles and bickering over asset-sharing and division that often takes place in traditional Indian business families. The more one has, the harder it seems to be able to share the munificence.

My daughters too had some difficulty in sharing things. Until . . .

I had taken my two daughters (then aged eleven and sixteen) to a Pizza Hut at the mall. We had an enjoyable dinner, each ordering a pizza of her choice. I couldn't finish mine; my youngest daughter clicked her tongue and spoke sternly (in perfect imitation of me), 'Now, now! No wasting. Eat up!'

Laughing, I asked for the remaining piece to be packed. On our way out, at the entrance of the mall, a group of four children—the oldest couldn't have been more than eight— ran to us with outstretched arms. I gave them a few coins. The eldest urchin, a girl, as emaciated as the others, looked longingly at the bag that I was holding. I hesitated for a split second: there was just one tiny slice and four famished mouths; the piece would hardly have sufficed for one, let alone four. With her outstretched hand coming closer to the bag I had no choice but to hand it over. She immediately peeked inside the bag and grinned. I played out the scene in my mind: she runs, the others chase; one succeeds in snatching bag; winner take all.

Then . . .

To my total amazement she took out the tiny triangular piece of pizza, broke it into four roughly equal parts and handed the others one each. When I looked at my daughters their faces bore the same look of amazement I was sure was on mine. It was a very quiet ride home.

Till that day I often had to act as mediator between my two girls, insisting they share their things from toys, chocolates, clothes, I-pod, etc. After that little incident outside the mall, without any lectures from me, my girls now amicably share whatever they have.

Anonymous

A Thousand Rupees

There is enough in the world to meet every man's need but not even one man's greed.
                                        Mohandas Karamchand Gandhi

'Could you give me a letter allowing a friend to stay for a month,' my maid, Heera, asked. She looked uncharacteristically anxious.

We lived in a defence colony which had strict security guidelines for allowing outsiders to stay. Heera was a verified member and lived in a small room close to our home. She had worked with us from the time we had arrived in Mumbai, and I knew we would miss her a great deal when we moved to another city, something that could happen anytime. Transfers were a part and parcel of an Indian defence officer's family after all.

This was the first time Heera had asked us to give her this kind of letter. *It must be important to her,* I thought, and completed the necessary formalities.

Her friend, Sona Bai, arrived soon after. I realised in a couple of days that she was partially blind. Yet, I could see her doing her best to be helpful by cleaning Heera's room. The month passed and Heera asked for Sona Bai's stay to be extended. This was a little difficult, but we managed to get the required permission.

It was then that I found out more about her. Sona Bai's eyesight had gradually failed and she had been supported by her daughter, her only living relative, for a few years. A few months back, her daughter had developed high fever and suddenly died. Sona Bai now had no one to call her own.

It was then that Heera had met her. Even with her limited means, Heera had not hesitated to immediately bring her home, though she was just a casual acquaintance. *Would I have been so large hearted?* I wondered. So called 'educated' people like us tend to think too much about long-term implications: 'How long can I keep her?', 'What will I do later?' and so on, and stop ourselves from a natural, human response; simple folk like Heera have much stronger values and courage.

Soon after getting Sona Bai's permission extended, I realised we needed to try and help Sona Bai settle down in a more permanent manner because of the colony's restrictions, and also because, once we moved, Heera might not be able to ask her next employer for permission.

However, this was easier said than done. Options were limited as blind homes in Mumbai could not take her in; they were already fully occupied and, besides, her case was weak as she was only partially blind. She was not old enough for an old age home. And her blindness did not allow her to take on the kind of job she could do earlier.

As I was pondering on what could be done, I got a call from one of the blind homes that I had approached in Mumbai. 'We understand the difficulty of the lady and have just got information that there is an ashram for the blind in Surendranagar in Gujarat, which has room for Sona Bai. Would you like to send her there?' the director asked.

This seemed suitable, but I wondered whether Sona Bai would want to move so far from her friends, and to a place where she did not understand the language. I spoke to her hesitantly and was amazed at her equanimity. 'God has opened yet another door for me,' she said calmly, 'yes, I shall go.'

We completed the formalities. Just before the social worker from the blind home came to take Sona Bai to Surendranagar, I gave Sona Bai a thousand rupees—a small amount, but enough to see her through for a couple of months at least.

When we got a call after three days from Sona Bai saying she had reached and was comfortable, I felt at ease and was happy that I could play a small role in making it possible for her to have a home.

There was one more surprise in store for me. The social worker called me in a few days saying she wished to meet me. Wondering what the matter could be, I went to meet her and was handed an envelope with a thousand rupees.

'Sona Bai asked me to give this to you,' the social worker said. 'And she asked me to write a letter to you on her behalf.' She opened up a sheet of paper, and read out:

'I am very happy here. We spend our time weaving and knitting. Thank you for finding this place for me. Please don't feel bad that I have returned your money. I took it thinking I might need it for travel or for some expense I might have in the ashram. But I spent nothing on travel. The social worker told me you had already paid for my ticket. When I reached here, I found I am given food and two sarees every year. What more do I need? The money is probably more useful to you. So, please take it back.'

The sheer courage of the woman and her perception of 'need' astounded me.

This remains the most precious thousand rupees I have ever received.

Jamuna Rangachari

Mirror Image

The calf walks briskly in front of us, tugging gently on the rope in my hands as if prompting me to walk faster. Today I'm with Sumitra, a spirited nineteen-year-old girl from the small Adivasi farming community of Kharia in Jhagadia district of Gujarat.

All of a sudden I feel a painful yank on the rope. I wince. Sumitra laughs.

'She knows the water hole is near and is in a hurry to get there. Release her, didi. She'll drink and scrounge around. Let us go this way.'

My eyes follow the direction she points. Cotton fields seem to extend endlessly in the distance, crowned by skies of azure.

I reach out my hand for Sumitra to hold as we climb gingerly downhill, kicking up dirt and rocks in the process. But it is not she who stumbles, I do. She tightens her grip on my hand, looks at me, and smiles. Her light brown eyes sparkle in the sun. Moments later, she turns excitedly towards me and points in the direction of the creek.

'Didi, did you see! Fish!'

As if on cue, tiny, frenzied fish materialise before my eyes, rushing hurriedly past each other in their underwater haven.

She throws a pebble into the water. They rush towards it.

'Let's try and catch one, didi.'

I roll up my pants in preparation for wading into the water. Sumitra takes off her dupatta, folds it in half, and holding it between her hands like an improvised sieve, wades into the water. She submerges her scarf. We wait in silent anticipation, hoping one will swim into the scarf. But the fish escape the makeshift net. We laugh at our underestimation of the task, wring out the dupatta and the bottoms of our pants, and start walking back home, hand in hand. Her warm, firm grip on my hand makes me smile. I hold her hand tenderly and hope that she doesn't let go. She doesn't.

'Didi, when people tell me that I'm not capable of something, I get really angry. It makes me want to show them that I can do anything.'

This is what strikes me most about Sumitra. One moment we're soaked to our knees trying to catch fish, laughing, acting silly, and in the next, she says something unexpectedly profound.

We're sitting and washing dishes outside in the dark, spoons clanging against cheap metal plates. She suddenly straightens her back, looks directly at me, and says, 'I don't want to get married. What promise does marriage hold? Marriage is self-ruin! I want to become something first, and then I'll get married. Not now. I want to do something first.'

In the midst of breaking twigs in preparation for the cooking fire, she looks up, thinks for a moment, and says matter-of-factly, 'Fear is inevitable when we venture to do something significant. We can't, however, allow the fear to defeat us. If we harbour fear, then nothing is possible.'

But Sumitra isn't just full of empty words. She acts. During the adolescent workshop held in Kharia, she noticed that a few girls couldn't read or write. When I suggested she start a class for these girls, she didn't just go home and think about it. She spoke to her parents about the proposition, and offered to teach every Sunday with my help. Together, we now teach a very excited group of seven girls every Sunday.

Sumitra is my muse. Through her energy, through her promise, I feel rejuvenated. Her desire to do more, see more, and learn more pushes me to think, to act, to create spaces for her to grow, for us to grow. The simple act of listening to her empowers me, gives me strength when I feel disheartened. By pushing her to realise her potential, I push myself to see beyond what lies immediately in front of me, of her. In physics, the force I exert on my environment doesn't exist in a vacuum, it generates an equal, but opposite force. Sumitra is this 'normal force'. I believe in Sumitra, and in turn, I believe in myself. In her words, I hear my own. In her voice, I hear my own. My potential has become intimately intertwined with hers. I watch her growing, and I feel myself growing with her, walking forward with her, hand in hand.

Prerna Srivastava

4

ON DEATH
AND DYING

All disease is a means towards some new joy of health, all evil and pain a tuning of Nature for some more intense bliss and good, all death an opening on widest immortality.

Aurobindo

Healing Myself

We were a happy family like any other; I thought I had everything: a doting husband (we had been dating since we were sixteen and seventeen), a bright and handsome son, and a lovely daughter. My small tailoring unit—more a hobby than work—kept me creatively occupied for those few hours that my children were away. In short, I had no complaints from life. We were a close-knit family, sharing all our meals together, and I prided in the fact that I was my son's best friend. That year everything changed.

I came back from my studio one afternoon to find my room locked from inside. I tried opening it, but couldn't. My first reaction was that the door must have gotten jammed. Then I remembered that my son had asked me for my room keys that morning as I was making my way out to my workplace. I called my husband to ask whether my son was with him; he said he wasn't. With the help of my domestic staff, I broke open the door latch and saw the lifeless yet smiling body of my son . . . he had chosen death over life. He was just eighteen.

My son had always been of a cheerful disposition, I couldn't believe that he could do . . . that . . . to himself. For several minutes I truly believed he was playing the fool with me. Like someone who had lost her mind I kept asking him to stop his game, to come down . . . .

I don't know when reality sunk in. I'd known he was depressed, but would never have imagined that he was entertaining suicidal thoughts. I don't know how that one month post his death passed, but I do remember the invaluable support of my family and friends who did not leave me or my husband alone, even for a minute.

My son's smiling image flashed through my eyes constantly. I didn't know how to handle the pain, the loss, the vacuum which seemed to suck my whole being. I sought medical help and was put on pills to calm my nerves. Everything felt useless . . . if we carried on living, it was only because of our little girl.

Then my aunt, who visited me for the first time a month after my son's death because she could not bear to see me so grieved, gifted me a book titled *The World Beyond*. This was my first step towards accepting what 'is'. Ever since our son had passed away, my husband and I had innumerable questions as to where he would be . . . in heaven, in this very house with us. The book gave us answers and in its pages we could cry and release our loss little by little.

Six months passed and the pain, though bearable by now, was still very intense. I felt the acute need to stop my dependence on pills and I told my husband so. Interestingly, that very day, I was travelling in the car with him to go to an organisation where we were chief guests supporting the cause of the underprivileged. A thought struck me. I told him, 'There are many who support the physical misery, I want to help those who are emotionally undernourished. I want to start a suicide helpline.' With tears swelling up in my eyes, I said, 'Perhaps I cannot share someone else's grief, like no one can share ours, but I want to do my bit to see that no parent has to go through what we have ... losing a child in his prime.' As I said those words, I knew that I would no longer just be living for the sake of living; it would be like a new life. For the first time in six months I wanted to live not just for my daughter but another cause equally powerful. That day I gulped the last pill to help me handle my fraught nerves. My husband supported me fully. I went through my trainings, fulfilled the formalities and we started our suicide helpline, the first in our city. Today our unit is ten years old with doctors, psychiatrists, psychologists and prominent people of our society helping as volunteers. We have helped avert many thousands of deaths. As the count of lives saved through my helpline goes up, I let go a little of my sorrow, a little of the guilt I feel that I hadn't foreseen the step my son took. Every time our suicide helpline helps someone, I fulfil my promise to my son that anyone who calls me with suicidal thoughts has to battle me first before giving up. I know that my son is watching me and is proud of his mother. And I hope I will never let him down again.

Even today almost a decade and a half later, we still celebrate my son's birthday and even Rakhi with as much paraphernalia ... because we believe he is still with us in spirit, if not in person.

Anonymous

Light amidst Darkness

We were at the civil hospital, awaiting the completion of the post-mortem on my uncle's body. Just forty-seven, he had died in a road accident. We were all in a state of shock: this man, who had been smiling, talking to us just a couple of hours back, was now a lifeless body. None of us could bring ourselves to say anything. We sat there quietly, waiting for the formalities to get over so we could perform the last rites. We all had one thing on our minds: the unpredictability of life. We build, plan, fight, sulk, but death washes everything away in a flash!

The immediate task, however, was to cremate the body before sunset. The ward boy came out of the post-mortem room, flung his bloodstained gloves in one corner, withdrew a bidi from his pocket and started smoking. The blood on his gloves was that of our beloved; how nonchalantly he had thrown them away. But then, this was just a job for him, something he did day in and day out. Smoking was perhaps some way of surviving this gruesome work which employed him and provided bread and butter to his family. After he finished his cigarette he signalled to us, gesturing that everything was almost done and that we would get custody of the body soon.

It was then that I noticed a man walking past us. His clothes were in tatters, his hair long and matted, and his beard overgrown. His actions were those of a man who had lost his sanity. I asked the ward boy who he was; he told me that this man was a cleaner at the hospital who had indeed lost his sanity a couple of years ago after losing his entire family in a train accident. Since then he had made the hospital his home and was often seen wandering aimlessly in the vicinity.

I noticed that his legs bore marks of many wounds, fresh and old. It was then that a thought struck me. I had a spare pair of shoes lying in my car. I got the shoes from the car and headed straight to the man. I said, 'Bhai I want you to wear these shoes. Please extend your foot so that I can put them on you.' He stared at me with a blank expression. I repeated my request and displayed the shoes and pointed at his feet. As the meaning of my words sunk in he extended his foot towards me majestically . . . just the way a person would to a street shoe-polisher. I took his foot and slid the shoe on; it fit him perfectly. I then fit the other shoe. After this the man began to walk around. He took a few steps and then suddenly broke into a dance. His face, body, his entire being was celebrating the feel of the comfort of the soft canvas on his bruised feet!

Everyone turned to look at him and their first reaction was that of disgust. This was the post-mortem section in a hospital; bodies were being dissected here; people had just lost their loved ones; and here was this man who was celebrating a pair of shoes.

But slowly, his naïve happiness engulfed us, changed us all from within. For a while, each of us forgot our own pain and lost ourselves in the genuine delight of this man. How little a thing had made him happy! How unrestrained his expression of that joy was. And most importantly, there was the realisation that we could each heal our sorrow a little bit by just being a witness to his bliss...

Yes, life is full of pain, but even in our greatest trials there can be moments of great bliss. We only have to be ready to recognise them.

Jayesh Patel

Load Sharing

The phone rang; I looked around for someone to answer it. I hate picking up the phone; people talk too fast, and when they ask for Rakesh, Ramesh, or Rajesh, I always end up handing it to the wrong person. But, that day, there was nobody else around and so I was forced to pick it up. It was a voice I recognised, Arvind's brother, calling to say that Arvind's one-year-old son had just expired.

There was a flurry of movement. Within ten minutes everyone in the office knew what had happened. We piled into a jeep and set off for Arvind's home to pay our respects. We sat in silence. I thought about how I didn't actually know what 'to pay respect' meant. I had known people who knew people that had died, but I had never been with someone whose grief was so fresh.

Unsure of which house was Arvind's, we zigzagged through the neighbourhood for a bit until we saw a line of men standing sombrely, facing the entrance to a home. That was the house. As women, we were allowed to go into the house, and so we took off our shoes and entered.

Inside were some thirty women who sat on the floor with their arms gently touching one another, their faces full of so much sorrow that my heart felt like it might break. It didn't matter that I, and some of my colleagues, had never actually met the child or his mother. It didn't matter that the baby had been mentally and physically disabled, and that there were whispers that this was for the best. This is what mattered: a one-year-old boy, wrapped in paper, lay lifeless in his grandmother's lap, his mother by her side, devastated.

We did the only thing we could. We sat together, and we cried together. We did this because maybe if we each took a little bit her sadness, there would be less for her to carry.

When the child's mother starts sleeping again, when enough time has passed that she can bear to think back to that day, she won't remember who came and who didn't. She won't remember what anybody said or what anybody brought. But she will remember that her house was full and that she wasn't the only one weeping.

This is our power—to feel each other's pain, and to collectively be a source of strength.

Tanya Sehgal

The Happiest Day of My Life

Happiness is a taste of success in the battle of life. For some it is glory, for others glamour; I am writing about an incident, when for me it meant contentment.

My younger brother's death on 20 June shocked me to such an extent that I could barely find a way out of my sorrow. I was so overcome with grief that I could not pay attention to anything: studies, school, friends . . . . I was angry at God for taking my brother away from me. He meant so much to me, that his memories would torture me even in my sleep. I couldn't perform any of the daily activities and couldn't understand this sense of meaninglessness that engulfed me completely.

It was my birthday on the 16th of August and by then my anger at God had reached its peak. I shut myself in my room and screamed at Him. It was as if my hatred towards Him was beyond my control and I had gone berserk.

Suddenly, a much longed-for fragrance filled the air. I felt two small arms embracing me. My brother was with me then . . . . God had fulfilled my longing.

Till date nothing has equalled that happiness which I felt for those fleeting, yet unforgettable moments.

Hridesh Kedia

My Angel

I was almost thirty-five and the journey so far had been a rigorous one. En route I had lost almost all my loved ones, one after the other. It started when I was sixteen, and I lost my dog. My brother had brought him home as a pup when I was about seven years old. I and the pup grew up together. In fact my brother, who had shifted to Mumbai a year after gifting me the pup, would joke whenever he came home that we both were trying to outdo the other in height. This childhood friend I lost, and that was my first jolt.

Then I turned seventeen and I lost my father. Things changed a lot both emotionally and financially. My mother and I shifted to Mumbai to be closer to my brother. There were a lot of ups and downs; my guiding force through it all was my mother. She taught me to cope up with everything. I finished my studies and took up a nice job. My brother too stepped up the ladder of success steadily. Financially things started changing. But before we could settle into a life of comfort, I lost my sister-in-law and then, within two years, my brother. My mother, strong as a rock, took the reins in her hands and started taking care of his two young sons and, of course, me too. Within five years I lost my mother to a massive heart attack. In her last days she had started saying that she was tired and that I should take care of things. All along I had known that she was putting up a brave front; facing the death of a child is heartbreaking for any mother. It was the two small boys who had made her hang on. And I hung on to the hope that as long as the two boys needed her she would fight. She tried her best, but finally it was beyond her to change fate.

The passing away of my mother killed a part of me emotionally. I was rudderless, and the responsibility of two boys who were just thirteen and eight seemed like a huge task to me. The kids would complain that I had changed, that I did not laugh with them anymore. It was true: I just couldn't enjoy the small things in life; I would laugh with people but without any genuine happiness. It all felt strange, scary at times. A simple matter of eating was ridden with guilt: I would think, 'How can I go on living when the others are gone.' I would sit in a corner of the room, looking out of the window, gazing far away into the horizon. Life had become a series of chores. I was living to complete my responsibilities. But thanks to all those dear friends who found time from their busy schedules and made me feel wanted, I continued to pull on.

Then one evening as I was returning from work with my younger nephew, a kitten—about two-three months—followed us to our lift. My nephew leapt with joy, 'Bua, a kitten! See, it's so pretty.' As we waited for our lift, a big cat came up to the kitten. My nephew was worried that it might hurt the young animal. Since I was getting late and I had various chores at home waiting, I assured my nephew that the cat wouldn't do anything. We got into the lift and I forgot all about it. The next morning the same nephew went out to water the plants and there, the same kitten came rushing up the stairs, meowing. And before he could close the door it was inside the house. Unconcerned, it walked into our hall and happily sat itself on my mother's favourite chair. No matter how much we tried, it refused to go out of the house. Thinking it was hungry I gave it some milk to drink and, in order to lead it out of the house, I placed the saucer outside the main door. It refused to go out. For some time we all sat on the stairs, trying to get it out of the house. The clever thing sat inside the house and kept gazing at us, its big black eyes wide open.

My nephews had been after me for quite some time to bring home a pet but I had refused, because I knew the pain of losing them. But that day, giving in to this obstinate kitten and their pleading, I agreed to let them keep her; they were thrilled. Equally thrilled was she, and as if she had understood, she leapt up with joy and trotted off to explore the other rooms. The house already belonged to her.

The first thing we did was to name the kitten and we decided on Rani. Today, she is the queen of the house in the truest sense. As a child I had read of fairy tales and angels who fulfil wishes. I'm convinced Rani is my angel, that her entry in our life was ordained by some higher power. Our apartment is at the farthest end from the main gate of the building. And, we are on the sixth floor. This makes my house the penultimate one in the society. Why didn't she choose to go to any of the other houses? To add to the list of coincidences, when I took her to the vet for her first vaccine, he had to put her date of birth on the certificate. He calculated it taking into consideration that she looked three months old at that time. And the date he calculated was the day my father had expired. They say that, after they pass away, our forefathers stay around us and as spirits take care of us. Rani's coming home has reinstated my belief.

Rani came at a time when I needed it the most; she brought life to my household. Her affection helped me rediscover life. I do sometimes get sad, of course, but she is always around to cheer me up with her demands. As Rani enriches our lives, I thank God for taking care of us when we needed it the most.

Sapna Bhattacharya

Sunny Side Up

One Saturday evening in April '98, we were entertaining friends at home. The topic of discussion was our forthcoming vacation to the hills. Suddenly my wife, Sheela, complained of a shooting pain in her abdomen. A gastric disorder, I said, and gave her an analgesic. The next morning the pain had become worse. We paid a visit to our family physician and with it began a flurry of sonographs, blood tests, and eventually endoscopies. On the fifth day we were told she had intestinal cancer.

Our oncologist suggested surgery. On the sixth day after the first pains Sheela was admitted to a hospital and operated. But the surgeons were aghast to see how rapidly the cancer had spread. They sewed her up without doing anything. One of the surgeons said to me, 'I am sorry but it is impossible to operate on her as the cancer has spread to almost the entire intestine and even the back wall of the stomach. Chemotherapy should be started immediately.' Softly, I asked, 'How much time does she have?' He said, 'About four months . . .'

We started her chemotherapy and I started my research on the internet. I went to hundreds of cancer research sites and finally took a four-hundred page print-out, from the Cancer

Research Institute, US, which detailed how one should deal with intestinal cancer. I also spoke to one of the best oncologists in the world today, Dr Bharat Bariya, who is based in the US. He was very kind and sent me about ten points to observe so as to delay the spread of the cancer as much as possible.

As an antidote to the burning caused by chemotherapy, my wife was put on grape juice, iron supplements, and lots of cold fluids. We also started many alternative therapies, one being ayurveda.

This went on for about three months. Then our family physician suggested we again consider surgery. Sheela and I discussed the matter. She said, 'I want to fight this. I will do my best. I need to get my daughter married, need to help my daughter-in-law with her delivery. I cannot go now, Shrenik. We must fight this out together.'

We went to Mumbai and went through another round of tests. To everyone's surprise there seemed to have been a remission of the cancer. In their terms it was a miracle. What had helped her? Chemo? Ayurveda? Her own will power? Her sunny side? Perhaps a combination of them all. While in Mumbai we went to three leading oncologists. All suggested surgery, but one said, 'Go to a bold doctor, not an old doctor, for that's what her case requires.' Sheela was adamant she be operated in her home town Ahmedabad, where family and friends would be around.

After long discussions, we found a doctor who agreed to perform this very complicated major surgery. He said, 'I can make an attempt, but cannot guarantee anything.' And then he asked me to get the patient. I said, 'Sir, this is the patient, sitting in front of you.' The doctor said, 'After so many sessions of chemotherapy patients hardly leave the bed. Sheelaben I am with you.' My wife said, 'Doctor, I am going to live, you go ahead in the way you think best.'

The surgery was successful. But about three days after the surgery Sheela started bleeding internally and had to be operated again. Another major surgery. When she regained consciousness, the doctor told her, 'Sheelaben you went through two major surgeries in the course of a week but you fought very well.' With an ever smiling face she said, 'Oh doctor, everything in my life happens twice. Two sets of tests, two surgeries . . . I know this is my second life.'

With this started one of the most beautiful phases of our life. Our daughter married, delivered her children, my daughter-in-law had hers. We vacationed, went on pilgrimages, celebrated festivals with more enthusiasm than ever before. Of course Sheela still had to have regular sessions of chemotherapy and had to undergo intermittent tests.

Three years later she developed another tumor, this time in her food pipe. She was operated again, but now the cancer was in an advanced stage. Moreover, she had become very weak physically, fighting against the intestinal cancer. She was put onto fresh chemotherapy; this time both of us knew it was now a matter of time.

One evening she said, 'Shrenik, you are going to spend a lot on my last rites. Instead, why don't we use the money to go to Palitana with the entire family; it's something that I would enjoy too.' Forty of us, my brothers, her brothers and sisters and their children went to Palitana and spent two most memorable days there.

The day before she passed away she said, 'Shrenik, God has been so kind to me.' *Kind?* I thought. She had suffered so much; she had been through hell with more than eighty-six cycles of chemo. My eyes watered. She continued, 'The doctors gave me four months but I lived for six-and-a-half years. These years were so beautiful, more than the forty before that put together. I am so lucky to have such people around me, a doting husband, loving children, friends, relatives, my mother (her mother was seventy-nine then, and had stayed with us during the entire last one-and-a-half year). Everyone has been so kind, so loving . . . what more could I have asked for?' One of the last things she said was, 'I have done everything that I desired and now I want to go.'

As she said those words I saw the shooting pain which she could not mask this time. I told her, 'Yes, we have had a wonderful life together. Thank you for showing me the sunny side up . . . always.'

Shrenik Shah

A Step to Living with Pride

It is almost twenty years today, but it seems like just yesterday. On 2 December 1987, I received news of the demise of my husband. He was chief electrical engineer in Indian Railways on deputation with RITES and had gone to Iraq for an inspection in October 1987.

I had given up my teaching job in April to venture into a business of my own on my husband's encouragement. I was on my way to becoming a successful entrepreneur when this tragedy struck.

The first thing that happens when death strikes a family is the assembling of relatives. In the midst of all the thronging relatives, the fact that my father-in-law was there meant a lot to me. He had been visiting us quite regularly after my marriage and was well aware of my nature and emotional make-up. I found solace and comfort in his presence. His eyes mirrored the heart-break and grief in mine.

In the north of India, as per tradition, a 'kriya' ceremony takes place on the thirteenth day after a person's death. On this day, prayers are recited in the gurudwara; after this, the widow is made to sit facing the Holy Book, and all the relatives and close associates put money in her lap. Such a tradition may have begun with good intentions to help a grieving family tide over a period of financial difficulty and bereavement. It was perhaps a method to ensure that a 'helpless' widow did not have to look beyond the family for sustenance and help.

The day before the kriya ceremony, a conference with this issue in mind began in earnest in my house. My mother, brothers and sisters started discussing 'how much they could afford to give me' at that time. I overheard my mother arguing for 'more money' for me. I was shocked and hurt beyond belief. I felt as if somebody was trying to humiliate me and strip me of all my self-respect and dignity.

My thoughts went back to the times I had spent with my husband. I had lived the life of a queen, enjoying all the comforts and facilities given to the family of a gazetted officer. Though we were not extremely rich, there was no shortage of anything. Both of us earned well, and we had two lovable, intelligent sons. It had been a perfect and idyllic family life, unmarred by tragedies or vicissitudes till now.

Because I was well qualified, I always managed to get a job as a teacher in a college or school every time my husband was transferred. My husband once told me, 'You are well qualified. Even if something happens to me, you will not have to go to anyone with a begging bowl. You can lead a life of dignity. I know you are an extremely sensitive and self-respecting person.' His words now resounded in my ears.

I barged into the room where the discussions were taking place.

'Mother,' I cried, 'this is just not done. You know I will never take this kind of help from anyone.'

'It is not your business,' my mother shouted at me, 'you cannot interfere in such things.'

'But it concerns me and my life and I shall not let it happen. I cannot imagine getting alms from others,' I shouted back.

My mother was in no mood to listen to me and continued with the discussion. I came out of the room and went straight to my father-in-law. He had always been my friend and supporter, one who acknowledged my emotions, spirit and convictions. I spoke my mind out to him. He listened very carefully and assured me that everything would be done according to my wishes.

The evening before the kriya ceremony, after the prayers—attended by family members, relatives and friends—my father-in-law said he wanted to make an announcement. Being an elderly and knowledgeable person in the family, my father-in-law commanded a high degree of respect.

There was silence while he spoke.

He said, 'As per the tradition, after the demise of the father, a turban is tied on the oldest son after the final prayers at the gurudwara on the thirteenth day. This custom is to declare that, after the father's death, the eldest son is the head of the family. We shall perform the ritual now in the house and not in the gurudwara.'

In the now shocked stillness of the gathering, he continued to speak.

'Our daughter,' he said, referring to me, 'is an educated person and is in a position to take care of the family. That is why I do not want anyone to offer her any money in the gurudwara, as is the custom. She is our daughter and if at all she needs any help, we do not have to make a show of it. In the privacy of our house we can help her. We must respect her feelings and I do not want any such ritual to be followed tomorrow after the prayers.'

His words stunned everyone. No one had the courage to speak out. They knew that I had a role to play in this, but had to maintain a respectful silence.

Everyone in the family knew that I was a rebel in my own way, but no one expected that, at this juncture of my life, I would take such a stand.

On 15 December 1987, the thirteenth day after my husband's death, the evening prayers were conducted in the gurudwara.

I did not wear white, as is customary for a widow in mourning. I decided to wear a green salwar suit that my husband had bought for me just before he left for Iraq. After the evening prayers, there was no ritual of tying a turban on my son's head. I was also not made to undergo what would have been the most humiliating experience of receiving alms in my lap at the gurudwara.

That was my first step towards my living the rest of my life with pride.

My brother was the first one to speak words of appreciation for breaking this shackle of humiliation. Many more were to follow later on. Today I am appreciated for handling my life independently and leading a life of self-respect and dignity in the absence of my husband.

As told to Abha Iyengar

5

OVERCOMING OBSTACLES

But difficulties were made to be overcome and if the Supreme Will is there, they will be overcome.

Aurobindo

A Drive to Dance

Sudha Chandran started dancing when she was three, and because she so evidently loved it, her father, an employee of the American Centre in Mumbai, took her when she was five to a famous dance school in the city. The teachers at Kala Sadan were reluctant to take on such a young girl, but Sudha's father requested the principal of the school to at least see the child dance before making a final decision. The principal was surprised to see Sudha perform so beautifully and agreed to admit her in the prestigious institution.

Sudha practiced with much zeal and dedication, and she gave her first dance performance on stage at the age of eight. By seventeen, she had presented seventy-five stage programmes, and received two important awards: the *Nritya Mayuri* and *Nav Jyoti*.

Then on 2 May 1981, when Sudha was travelling in a bus to Tiruchi temple along with her parents, there was an accident. Her bus collided with a truck, killing the driver on the spot and injuring several passengers, including Sudha. She was immediately taken to the nearest hospital. Here, the doctor made a mistake. He plastered her right leg, which had been injured; if it had been left open, the gangrene that eventually set in could have been prevented. After a few days, Sudha noticed that the colour of her skin on the leg was changing. After examination that doctors concluded that her leg had developed gangrene. In order to save her life, the leg had to be amputated seven-and-a-half inches below the knee.

Sudha remained in a state of shock for some time. Slowly, however, it dawned on the young dancer that things could have been much worse. That was the turning point that put her on the road to recovery. She began meditating, something that helped her realise that the strength to overcome what had happened lay within her; she just needed to bring it out.

Gradually her confidence returned and she began walking with the help of a wooden leg and crutches. In the meanwhile, she continued her studies in Mumbai. One thing she was uncomfortable about was the pity with which her friends looked at her. The only way she could make them stop, she felt, was if she started dancing again. She chanced upon an article on Dr P.K. Sethi who had been awarded the Magsaysay for having invented the Jaipur foot, a solid, flexible prosthetic foot. Sudha wrote to him, and he immediately replied, asking her to visit Jaipur. When Dr Sethi examined Sudha's amputated leg, he assured her that she would be able to walk again normally. Will I be able to dance again, Sudha asked. 'Yes, why not?' the doctor promptly replied.

Dr Sethi took up the job as a challenge. He used aluminium for the foot and fashioned it in a way that allowed it to rotate easily. A new round of struggle began for Sudha. First, she began to practice walking, and then to dance. This was not easy. Although Dr Sethi deputed an assistant to study Sudha's dance movements so he could accordingly make changes to the foot, not all the problems could be removed. Her leg would often bleed and as the movements of the leg become faster, the pain became more severe. However, Sudha's deter-mination did not falter.

Finally, once she had mastered all the dance positions, she decided that she would perform on stage once again. On 28 January 1984 two thousand people thronged a hall meant for five hundred to watch Sudha dance. At the end of the performance, the hall echoed with the sound of applause.

Sudha's story inspired the famous Telugu film producer Ramoji Rao to bring out a film based on her life story. The film was titled *Mayuri* and Sudha herself was cast as the protagonist. Over the years, Sudha has gone on to become to popular actress in television.

Of her experience, Sudha once said, 'In my hour of agony and loss, I had the choice of swimming against the tide or drowning. I chose to swim and swim hard.'

Tapti Rajaram

Beautiful Life

*The question why there is evil in existence is the same as
why there is imperfection . . . . But this is the real question
we ought to ask: is this imperfection the final truth, is evil
absolute and ultimate?*

Rabindranath Tagore

I met Johnny Lever when I was working on my book on
parenting. The story of how this renowned comedian grew
up in a slum, where he earned a living selling vegetables, and
in his free time made people laugh with his wisecracks, moved
me. He made his debut in the film *Yeh Rishta Na Toote*, and
there was no looking back. But there was a point, he told me,
living in Dharavi, when he had considered ending it all. This
is what he said:

I was about twelve then. Tired, frustrated and depressed
with the violence, poverty and hopelessness that I saw all
around me every single day, I decided to end it all by ending
my life. Dharavi, a little India by itself, had people from every
province and state who had migrated to this dream city

Mumbai to make it big but had instead ended up in this, the most violent, harsh, filthy slum, the largest slum in Asia. Living here defied the very essence of humanity. Jungle Raj prevailed and might was always right.

As usual that evening too my father came home drunk and started abusing my mother, verbally and physically. I saw the helplessness in her eyes, and to save both of us pain and embarrassment, walked out from our five feet by five feet dwelling which was 'home' to five of us. Without even my realising it, my feet took me towards the railway tracks. Even today I vividly remember how little I felt as I walked on the cold metallic track. I saw a train approaching furiously towards me, but within me everything was dead. I said to myself that even death could not be worse than the life I was living. I continued to walk towards the train. Then, with the train just a few seconds from me, the image of my sisters and my mother flashed before my eyes. What would happen to them once I was gone? What if they too took the same path? I could do this to myself, but could I do this to them? I got off the tracks.

Though I had got over the impulse of the moment, I was still depressed and hurting within. I went and sat behind a makeshift box-type salon, so typical a sight in any slum, with my head in my hands thinking, *what now*? It was then that I heard this beautiful piece of music playing on the radio in the salon. It was a song by Lata ji. Her melodious voice engulfed all my pain and for some time I was aware of nothing but the beauty of the lyrics, and the voice of the singer. The voice was healing me, soothing me, comforting me. I sat there for more than two hours, enjoying the beauty of music, and I realised that if there is pain in this life, there is healing too. If there is hopelessness, there is hope as well. If there is ugliness, there is beauty. That day, I knew that I would never give up on this gift called life.

Johnny Lever
As told to Raksha Bharadia

Facing Adversity

Sometimes it takes years for something to change your life. And sometimes, it takes only moments for everything in your life to change. Though it happened almost two decades ago, the sequence of events is crystal clear even today.

After several hours of preparing an array of snacks for my son's fifth birthday party the next day, I had joined the small group of women and children living in the colony for a well-deserved break. We were about half a dozen families staying there, besides a few officers who had opted to leave their loved ones back home. Baghdad in 1988 was not really the safest of places to live in—even though the Iraq-Iran war was coming to a rather drawn out end. Once in a while, a missile from across the border would contribute a bit of unwanted excitement to life. In contrast, viewing films brought from India in our makeshift clubhouse provided a more favoured source of entertainment.

Watching a typical Bollywood tearjerker that evening, I shed copious tears—but from just one eye. To cover up my embarrassment, I smiled more than required during the post-mortem of the story—a regular feature after every film. I didn't realise I had gone rather overboard in my efforts until one of the older children commented on it!

It was only when we sat down for dinner that it occurred to me that something was not quite right. Putting the first spoonful of food in my mouth, not only did I spill some of it, but I found it abnormally difficult to chew or swallow what little made it into my mouth. The decision to wash it down with water was easier to make than execute: drinking proved equally complicated, the water dribbling down the side of my mouth. As the front of my kurta became wet, fear insidiously crept into my heart. 'I think my face is paralysed,' I remember announcing rather dramatically. Only to be reproved by my husband, who ticked me off for my fertile imagination. Finally, however, he was persuaded to call the in-house doctor, a fellow Indian who fortunately lived in the same colony, who abandoned his half-eaten dinner and came immediately. Though the doctor suspected a problem, he rather cautiously decided to refrain from making any diagnosis till the next morning.

It was a very long night and the little sleep I managed to get was fitful. And next morning, we didn't have to wait for the doctor to confirm that something was certainly wrong. I discovered it was difficult to speak—my mouth felt as if it was stuffed with food. When I managed to utter a few words, even I couldn't understand what I said. My face looked distorted: there seemed to be a permanent lopsided smile pasted on it and my lips were practically halfway up my left cheek. My left eye had a tendency to water, without the help of any emotional trigger. It could have been because the eyelid had apparently lost its ability to shut. Like some tiny spring suddenly gone out of order. My ability to eat or drink had deteriorated drastically as well—something that became apparent when I tried to have breakfast.

Neither my husband nor I had ever heard or seen such strange symptoms. With a premonition of disaster, we waited for the doctor to arrive and put a name to the strange condition. And when he informed me that it was Bell's Palsy—a fancy-sounding name for facial paralysis—I couldn't resist telling my husband, 'I told you so!', despite my garbled speech.

The first of my many trips to the hospital in Baghdad was unforgettable. The sights were more or less familiar—waiting ambulance, the rush of patients, crowded wards, stretchers and wheelchairs—and so was the smell—antiseptic and medicinal. But the sounds were completely alien—incomprehensible language, totally foreign tone and pitch. We must have had some tie up with the hospital as our doctor seemed quite at home in the surroundings.

The line of treatment was worked out and started immediately. The daily injections were not too bad. A jab and it would be over, never mind if parts of my anatomy resembled a pincushion very soon. But it was the so-called physiotherapy that turned out to be quite a nightmare. Because it transpired to be anything but sessions of gentle pulls and pushes. Made to sit on a not-so-comfortable, hard-backed chair, I waited as our doctor—short and thin—discussed the finer details of the therapy with the hospital doctor, a local Iraqi who appeared huge in comparison. The conversation in broken English was liberally spiked with exclamations, in both Arabic and Hindi, and supplemented with lots of gestures. It was only when my hands were secured to the arms of the chair that the implication of the volts and minutes I had heard being mentioned sank in.

The electric volts given must have been minimal, but were painful nonetheless. Strapped and helpless, waves of self pity would wash over me as my eyes would fill with tears. The ten or fifteen-minute sessions appeared to last for hours. Trying to distract myself, irrational thoughts would cross my mind—like campaigning against capital punishment and the electric chair.

It was a long road to recovery. But I was determined to overcome this unwanted disability as quickly as possible. The fact that I had received medication immediately was in my favour. Never will I forget the young girl I had seen at the physiotherapy department very early in my treatment. Her face had been horribly distorted and I had imagined she too was a new case. The information that she had been coming for more than three months made me resolve to implicitly follow everything the doctor said.

The ability to adapt to any condition comes easy to us human beings! I learnt how to eat small morsels and avoid spilling. Mealtimes became slightly extended, but it gave the family more quality time together at the dining table. At least that is how we looked at it. Drinking with a straw made things easy—bless the genius who had invented it so thoughtfully. I even learnt the trick of shutting my left eye that would remain obstinately open—I just had to close the eyelid manually!

The paralysis had only affected the left side of my face. I was perfectly capable of doing everything else. Life slowly went back to the normal schedule—housework, movies, get-togethers. Everybody had been extremely sympathetic and helpful. And as the days turned into weeks, and the first signs of recovery started showing; there was no dearth of encouragement. But it took almost six months before I was back to normal.

Today, people can't discern any facial deformation. And when I mention those traumatic months—which is very rare—their surprise is evident. That's because Bell's Palsy taught me the value of smiling all the time. Smiles that immediately erase the faint trace of distortion I can see in the mirror. Smiles that hide my triumph over adversity. Smiles that convey my happiness and contentment. Smiles that reiterate that it is indeed a beautiful world.

Anjana Jha

Faith and Perseverance

Ahmedabad, 26 January 2007. Like the rest of India I too was enjoying the Republic Day holiday. Thankfully, there had been no emergencies. Being a gastrointestinal surgeon I was used to half-eaten meals and parties left mid-way because of emergency calls.

My mobile rang around eight in the evening. Apparently a police inspector, Nikunj, had met with an accident and was in a hospital at Rajkot. The doctor attending him was on the line. Nikunj had suffered major organ failure and had very low blood pressure; his lungs were not functioning and he was on a ventilator; his kidneys had failed and he was undergoing dialysis.

It seemed a lost cause to me; I wondered if it made sense for me to drive up to Rajkot in the middle of the night and told the reporting doctor so. It was then that the wife of the patient, Dhirajben, herself a nurse, came on the line. She requested me to drive down. I still remember her words, 'Sir, I know he requires immediate surgery and I know you can do it. His condition is very serious, but if you think that there is even one percent chance of him making it I would like to take it. I don't mind if you operate and he dies, but it is only with you that I want to take my chances.'

Her faith in me and her positivism in what seemed to me a hopeless situation touched me. I drove down to Rajkot and we operated the whole night. Nikunj showed signs of improvement soon and we shifted him to Ahmedabad. But soon after his condition started deteriorating.

We did a second operation within the first week of the first surgery. He did well for a few days and again started deteriorating. One after the other, within a span of three months, we performed ten major abdominal surgeries on a man who was on a ventilator with major organ failure.

Every time he would deteriorate and require another surgery, I would talk to Dhirajben. Unflinchingly she would say, 'Sir, no problem. Go ahead.' A time came when we could actually predict when he would start deteriorating. It was as if every week he followed a cycle. After each surgery he would respond positively for the first three to four days, and then start deteriorating. It was a very strange phenomenon. In my entire medical career I had neither heard of nor treated such a case.

After his seventh surgery questions started nagging me.

Am I justified in operating again and again? Is there any sense to this? The family was paying through its nose—how were they managing the costs? They were a middle-class family, not crorepatis.

In this pessimistic frame of mind I spoke to Dhirajben, 'I am not sure how long we can go on like this....' A bright smile lit up her serene face. She replied, 'Do not worry sir, you do your best. If you feel he requires another surgery, go ahead and operate.'

Dhirajben was a nurse. She understood well enough the seriousness of the entire situation. Yet she retained her faith. She continued to believe that doing our best is the most that we all can do. The quiet strength of her faith and perseverance gave me the courage to continue struggling, and with renewed effort.

Nikunj spent five full months in the ICU before he finally went home. Yes, he is weak; but gaining strength everyday.

With Dhirajben at his side I know he has the best chances that anyone can ever have.

Sanjiv Haribhakti

Healing through Music

The sun slowly sets over dusty Ahmedabad as I teach tabla to a small group of slum children under the aegis of Manav Sadhana. Through the smog, the refracted sun rays set the languid Sabarmati river afire.

Rajiv's seven-year-old eyes shimmer as he approaches the group. They glow so radiantly that they draw attention away from his ragged clothes and the dust covering his face. He announces to the group, 'I want to learn tabla too.' The group of boys and girls sitting around me makes space for him in the circle. I guide them while they vocalise the basic bols on the drums, accenting specific notes to create rhythmic melodies.

Dha	*te*	*te*	*dha*	*te*	*te*
1	*2*	*3*	*1*	*2*	*3*

We recite aloud in unison, and they clap to the rhythm. Some of them close their eyes, trying to feel the beat.

Rajiv catches on quickly, and soon, volunteers to try the rhythm. He sits down in front of me, beaming with confidence, ready to share what he has learnt. The group silently watches and waits. While he begins to play, I adjust his hands and posture to help him produce the right sound and resonance. He eagerly responds, and his face turns from joy to intense concentration back to joy as the challenge and pleasure of playing the tabla sink in.

While he plays, I look at his hands, and notice severe burns in some places. His tiny wrists and forearms are discoloured and bruised. 'Beta, what happened to your hands?' I ask Rajiv gently. His eyes are closed, and he is concentrating on the beat. It takes him a minute to realise that I just asked him a question. He explains, 'I help my father fill bottles with cleaning agents to sell on the streets. Sometimes, the liquid spills and burns my hands. After the riots, we had to find work. This is how we make money.' Looking more carefully at his hands, I see that the burns are from corrosive liquids. The realisation numbs me, but soon a smile emerges on his face.

'Tabla is hard but fun!' he proclaims. The others there erupt into laughter too. I smile with them, realising that music for this child is a means to heal, to overcome the difficulties of his present situation. It is pure joy for him, for me, and for the group.

Nine months later, I find myself sitting again on the stone pavilion gazing out over the dry Sabarmati river bed. I returned to Manav Sadhna on behalf of Project Ahimsa to implement new grants and check on the progress of our existing music programmes. The sun is relentless, heating the black spot on my tabla. I am practicing a Lucknow composition, taught by my guru, Pandit Swapan Chaudhuri. The bell-like resonance of the notes attracts a group of children, and Rajiv is among the group. He quickly runs to sit beside me, intently listening to me practice. He smiles, opens his mouth to say something, then stops. When I pause to adjust a setting on the tabla he speaks: 'I have been practicing! Can I show you what I have learned?'

Surrounded by the other children who have followed him, Rajiv patiently and slowly plays a composition I taught him over nine months ago. The notes are clear and deliberate, and his recitation of the bols is remarkably clear. I learn from the other children that, since that day nine months back, Rajiv has been taking regular tabla classes and has developed a great love for music. And that, since then, he has also been much more interested in his maths and science classes. Rajiv informs me with sparkling eyes that his grades have improved greatly. I smile, looking forward to my next trip to India and my next lesson with Rajiv.

Robin Sukhadia

Hope's Daughter

She entered the room riding on the arms of a man, who deposited her into the waiting chair delicately, as if she were a piece of rare china. She smiled brightly at us, a smile warm enough to bring our voices back, though it didn't. We had reason enough to be nonplussed. The earlier occupants of the chair had been quite different. Daughters of tailors, mechanics and clerks from rural districts and small towns or from the city, who faced us edging their hope of a chance at higher education with a strange mixture of diffidence and confidence. Daughters of India with an ambition to become self reliant, dreaming of the means to research plant genes and find new pest-resistant strains of crops, or of competing for the civil administrative exams. Women who not only excelled in their studies but dared to hope for a life beyond the fringes. And were working to make that hope turn real. They had come one by one, dressed simply, hair combed into submission, eyes bright with anticipation and faced the questions we had posed.

But now, faced by this young woman in the chair, we suddenly had no questions. At least no questions polite enough to be asked. She broke the silence by telling us her name . . . Rameshwari. Polio had robbed her of her legs while she was still a child. But her father had supported her in her search for knowledge and she had passed school and college with flying colours, even distinction. And now, she told us, she hoped to complete an MBA course, the fee for which was more money than her family had seen in its entire lifetime to date. If we, the jury deciding on scholarships to the economically challenged, would find her deserving, she would be able to realise her dream.

We found our voices then, and asked her the first of what would end up as a battery of questions. What was her dream, we wondered aloud. 'To become CEO of a company,' she answered, without batting an eyelid. It seemed a dream indeed. This chit of a girl who had to be carried from place to place, what miracle would get her into a boardroom? 'I cannot settle for anything less,' she said, hearing our unasked query. 'You see, considering my handicap, that is the only way I can ensure I am taken seriously.'

She had it all worked out to the last detail. The grant, if she got one, would help her choose from the three colleges that had shown an interest in accommodating her as a student to their MBA course if she could pay the fees. And she would use some of the money to get herself a wheelchair, 'to free my brother from having to spend his day carrying me around, and allow him to find a job . . . he has a Bachelor's degree, you know,' she added proudly. She was sure her results would win her a placement with a company where she would work her way up 'with dedication and integrity' and finally head some organisation as its Chief Executive. 'I know I can do it,' she added, mistaking our silence for disbelief.

She told us a bit more about her family: her father a low grade government employee; her brother, who took up odd jobs so he could carry her to college and back home; her elder sister, married and settled in another town; and her mother, an unlettered housewife who fuelled the dreams of her three children to move beyond their boundaries; 'Everyone in my family believes I can make it,' she added, as at the end of the interview her brother came to pick her up and carry her away.

We stared at one another after they had gone, humbled and awed. And prayed that nothing would sour her dream. We sent her a letter, congratulating her on the grant of the scholarship for her study course and her wheelchair. I could not help sending a note of my own with a request. That when she finally got into her office as CEO, I should be the first journalist to interview her about her vision for the company she headed.

Sathya Saran

Looking at Myself from Inside

When was the last time you looked at yourself? I don't mean in the mirror, I mean *really* looked at yourself from inside— where you are heading, what your lifestyle is. Most of us— and achievers in particular—are so busy running, coping and getting ahead, that we have no time to stop and look inward. Till our bodies force us to.

I remember the day in 1997 when I woke up in the middle of the night with a nasty pain shooting down my lower back. Over-exertion, I told myself. I'd had a speaking engagement in Mysore, a meeting in Delhi, and a seminar in Hyderabad that fortnight. I decided to take it easy for a couple of days.

The pain got worse. By the end of the month, I could barely walk without groaning. The general practitioner I went to could find nothing wrong, so he sent me to a gynaecologist, then to a urologist and an orthopaedic surgeon. I had x-rays done and was told I had a rare but simple problem of a pelvic bone that required rest and a surgical belt. I wore the belt and used a wheelchair but the pain got worse. Doctors suggested a bone scan.

All hell broke loose even before I got off the scanning machine (at a very prestigious hospital in Bangalore). The doctor told my daughter, who was waiting outside clutching a sheaf of x-rays, that the scan showed 'multiple metastases' (technical term for the spread of cancer cells), with large patches of skull, vertebral and pelvic bone damage. If the 'treatment' worked, the diagnosis said, I had 'eighteen months'. However, radiation would be tricky, as all vital organs were close to the damaged areas. My daughter began sobbing.

That was in March 1998. I came home in a daze, and on an impulse called an oncologist friend who immediately put me through a series of additional tests over the next three months—endoscopy, nuclear imaging, biopsies. Every single report was negative (except for the bone scan patches).The biopsies were painful, the daily running around for tests and the anxiety were as exhausting and traumatic as the back pain itself.

Eighteen months. If that. I began 'putting my affairs in order'..The previous ten years had been hectic—I had written six books, acquired two doctorates in sociology and music, taught abroad on an assignment, published over one thousand articles, taught music four times a week, and kept up my weekly columns even while travelling. I had straddled three careers, as journalist, musician and consumer activist, and enjoyed every moment, but now it was time to catch up with other things.

I did a round of banks to register nominations for fixed deposits. (I remember looking at receipts that matured in May 2000, and telling myself that I would be gone by that date.) I wrote a will, filed receipts and documents, and called my editors to warn them I might have to be hospitalised.

When the first two biopsies were inconclusive, the doctors did a third, going deeper, and cutting a larger chunk of bone from my back, to get a good look at the damaged areas. (At this rate, I thought wryly, writhing in pain, I wouldn't have much pelvic bone left, damaged or healthy!) The third report too, was inconclusive. Finally, one doctor advised an open biopsy of the skull lesion, while another considered it too risky to drill through the skull, and advised opening the back. It could be Paget's Disease, one doctor said. We looked up Paget's on the internet but my test results did not fit in. I travelled to Tata Memorial Hospital in Mumbai for a second opinion. They too advised an open biopsy.

In the meantime, a friend talked me into trying reiki. Another took me to a gem therapist and homeopath, while another advised pranik healing. Yet another sent me an article on unconventional strategies for coping with pain. My sister-in-law took me to meet a friend who had been given up as a terminal case three years earlier but was now in perfect health after siddha vaidya treatment. It was a chaotic, disorienting time.

Another bone scan five months later showed the patches were exactly as before, neither larger nor shrunken. Baffled and thoroughly exhausted, I decided to cry a halt to the tests, promising the doctors that I would return if the pain worsened.

Two years passed, then three, four. I began travelling abroad again. I walked slower and accepted fewer engagements, but began looking at myself 'from the inside' as it were, stopping to assess each move, each goal, before deciding whether the glitter and gains were worth reaching for. Most of us don't have the time to do that. We run, frenzied, from one goalpost to the next, in pursuit of 'achievement', forgetting that nothing comes without a price. And that price may not be in terms of money.

According to the bone scan, I ought not to be on my feet. According to the other tests, there was nothing wrong with me. Except for the relentless pain. 'Madam,' one doctor said to me, during the third biopsy, 'your body refuses to behave according to our textbooks.'

Mull over that. We are bodies, not machines. And the best of doctors concede that they are merely getting closer, with each case, to a better (not a complete) understanding of how the human system works. Bone scan patches usually indicate malignancies. They do not know yet, why some bone scans show patches when other tests are negative.

One doctor is convinced that whatever was wrong with my body, my spirited, positive attitude helped trigger my auto-immune system and arrest the ailment. Maybe. The mind-body connection is now cited in more and more cases around the world, with a proven correlation between those who let themselves be devastated by a diagnosis of doom, and the progression of the illness. We have made progress in terms of mapping the genetic code, but mapping the land of the inner self is yet in the realms of the unknown.

I did a lot of book reviews while I was undergoing tests (there you are—I was deeply conditioned. by upbringing, to think that if I couldn't run around, I had to somehow use my time 'productively'). One of the books I reviewed was R.M. Lala's *Celebration of the Cells*, where he describes how he coped with cancer. 'I lived with the tyranny of the next thing to do,' he says. 'Even a walk became a task to do and get over with.' Does that ring a bell? Being 'busy' and 'overworked' conveys, in our modern way of life, status, importance, self-worth. Workaholism, rather than contentment and peace, is exalted.

When one's days are declared to be numbered, definitions of 'more pressing matters' get altered dramatically, whether it is getting down to writing that long-standing letter to a friend or visiting the orphanage down the road. These don't bring a byline or cheque, but they garner other kinds of non-quantifiable returns.

My case shows that, despite diagnoses, there is always room for hope. Because bodies 'don't always behave according to textbooks'. The BBC ran a programme about a man who had lost all body sensations at nineteen, couldn't lift a spoon to his mouth, couldn't speak, and was declared incurable. Today he is walking, working and leading a normal life. There is no medical explanation.

Sakuntala Narasimhan

The Butterfly

A man found a cocoon. One day a small opening appeared; he sat and watched the butterfly for several hours as it struggled to force its body through the little hole. Then it seemed to stop making any progress. It appeared as if it had gotten as far as it could and could go no farther. So the man decided to help the butterfly.

He took a pair of scissors and snipped the remaining bit of the cocoon. The butterfly could now emerge from the cocoon easily. But something was odd. The butterfly had a swollen body and shrivelled wings. The man continued to watch the butterfly, because he expected that at any moment, the wings would enlarge and expand to be able to support the body, which would contract in time. Neither happened. In fact, the butterfly spent the rest of its life crawling around with a swollen body and deformed wings. It was never able to fly.

What the man in his kindness and haste did not understand, was that the restricting cocoon and the struggle required for the butterfly to get through the small opening of the cocoon are nature's way of forcing fluid from the body of the butterfly into its wings so that it is ready for flight as soon as it emerges from its cocoon. Sometimes struggles are exactly what we need in our lives. If nature allowed us to go through all our life without any obstacles, it would cripple us. We would not be as strong as we could have been. Not only that, we could never fly.

Author Unknown

The Indomitable Spirit

When I called up Girish Gogia after a gap of four years, I dreaded to hear his voice; surely there would be defeat in it, after all, how much can the human spirit endure? I thought the battle he'd had to fight over the last few years must surely have robbed him of his spirit. So the cheerful voice on the other end of the phone surprised me. And the conversation that followed thereafter proved me completely wrong. It reflected the optimism that had left a deep impression on my mind when I had interviewed Girish as a journalist. While he excitedly talked about what was happening in his life, I remembered the incident that had confined him to a wheel chair.

It was the eve of the new millennium. Spirits was soaring high as a group of enthusiastic people from Mumbai reached Goa to bring in the new year. A friend of Girish's suggested they go to the beach. It was two in the afternoon. When they reached the beach, Girish decided to go into the sea. 'I'll be back soon Isha,' he said to his wife, waved to her, and ran towards the sea, diving into a high wave. Soon after, a cry was heard from where he had dived. 'Help! Girish is lying unconscious, please help!' It was Isha, who had run towards the sea as she did not hear her husband's jubilant voice soon after he had dived into the sea. Girish was rushed to the hospital. The next day, as the world celebrated the new millennium, Girish was declared paralysed as a result of severe spine injury.

That was eight years back.

'Tell me about your life,' I heard Girish's voice on the other end, transporting me into the present. 'I will tell you when we meet,' I answered as I felt a heavy feeling descending upon me. I could not easily forget how, in some of my darkest moments, I drew inspiration from him.

I remembered our first meeting, when this young, handsome man in his thirties, with a 'never-say-die' attitude and a disarming smile, had spoken so confidently about his convictions. He had refused to succumb to self pity and was determined to live life to the fullest. He had said, 'It is my body which is damaged and not my mind, and I'm thankful to God for that. If I sulk now, I would be insulting God for not admiring His beautiful creation.'

He had kept himself busy by watching his favourite channels, especially National Geographic and Discovery Channel, which would fuel his passion for knowledge. And in no time he had started moving out of the house in a wheelchair.

One day there was a hue and cry in the building complex he lived in. Girish wanted to convert the garage space to start an office to continue his business of interior decoration. This had met with opposition. 'Why can't you live and let live?' he had roared, eventually managing to convince everyone. After much struggle he landed himself an assignment to design a three bedroom flat. Girish executed it so efficiently that he landed another assignment. After that there was no looking back. The Railway authorities too contacted him and hired his services as a consultant to renovate the Churchgate and Bombay Central stations in Mumbai.

As the days passed, I felt an increasing admiration for Girish. There is one quality in him which has stood out despite all the odds. Then and even today, Girish has not stopped being rational and logical. He believes in God and has blended these two extremely well. That is why his faith in God and positivity, and his belief in the magic of nature and humanity, always leads him to strive harder. In the hope of walking one day he does eight hours of meditation every day, visualising himself walking and running. 'I have already started feeling positive changes in my body,' he told me when I met him after our phone conversation. His face and spirit both looked as young as ever. The passage of time had not dimmed the bright spark that fuelled his passions. 'Do you know how little medical science knows about our body?' he said. 'That is why I am not going to stop trying. So you will see me walk soon.'

Where is Isha? How is she? I enquired about his wife as I was leaving. 'Well, there is a bit of bad news. Isha was diagnosed with multiple sclerosis; she's fifty percent paralysed now,' he said matter-of-factly.

I was dumbfounded. I just touched his hand gently as he smiled that angelic smile which comes with not having lost hope.

Darshana Doshi

The Power to Change

If you thought that Mahatma Gandhi was one of the brightest students in his class, or one of the most outstanding student leaders in his youth, then you may be in for a surprise. Not only was he a mediocre student, he was a very quiet and shy teenager as well. But did that stop him from becoming India's 'Father of the Nation'?

No.

Gandhi's story teaches us that you can still create your own story of victory—just like he did.

Born into a middle class family, Mohandas K. Gandhi had low self esteem when he was young; because of this he seldom stayed back after school to interact with other classmates for fear of being ridiculed. That was also part of the reason for his early unhappiness in his marriage (when he was thirteen years old) as his young bride had difficulty accommodating his impatient, jealous and demanding outbursts.

He didn't do well in school either. After struggling to graduate from high school, he moved on to study medicine in a local university only to fail badly and, subsequently, was forced to quit. At that time, he had attended that university for only five months.

In their desperate bid to help the young man, his family decided to send him to England to study law, a course which they believed he would be able to cope with. They pooled all the financial resources that they could get and finally sent the excited Gandhi off to London to embark on a fresh new start.

A stranger in a foreign land, Gandhi had difficulty adjusting to the seasonal weather in London and would often be teased for his inappropriate seasonal attire and his poor command of the English language. To make up for all these, he worked very hard, trying to excel in both his studies and other curricular activities such as French, dancing, violin and elocution. Those proved to be short-lived as he found himself running out of money gradually. To cut costs, he gave up his hotel for a small room and walked instead of travelling on buses. He also changed his diet, switching English meals for simple vegetarian fare. Interestingly, these newly adopted lifestyle habits formed the basis of his lessons on health and simple living subsequently.

In India, due to his inadequate knowledge about Indian law, he had difficulty getting a case. And when he finally secured one, Gandhi had stage fright at the last moment and abandoned the courtroom abruptly, leaving his colleague to conduct the cross examination. It was a disgraceful debut.

His inability to succeed as a lawyer drove Gandhi back home again. With the help of his brother, Gandhi decided to go to South Africa and take up a clerical position there, leaving his wife and two sons back in India. But it wasn't smooth sailing in South Africa either. Instead of landing a clerical position, Gandhi realised that he had been engaged for a civil suit that required strong accounting knowledge and detailed legal analysis. This, and the harsh discrimination against Indians in the country, drove Gandhi into wondering whether he should leave South Africa or stay on to fight the case, until one day something happened.

While riding on the first class carriage on the train to another town, he was ordered to move to the freight compartment, although he had a ticket. When he refused, he was unceremoniously thrown off the carriage. As he waited in the station for the next available coach, thoughts of his present circumstances flooded his mind. It suddenly dawned on him that, despite changing his environment each time, he was unable to avoid the challenging issues ahead. He realised that it was cowardly of him to run away from his fears instead of helping the people to fight for the rights they deserve.

Gandhi then started working hard on the case, drilling into the details zestfully. With his diligence and perseverance, he learned a lot about the case and counteracted against the punitive nature of the lawsuit by persuading his client and the other party to settle on an amicable reconciliation out of court. His apt handling of the suit earned the respect of the Indian community, so much so that he was asked to delay his departure back home to help them in another case to fight for the rights of Indian settlers in the country. That catalysed his involvement into politics. He would eventually propose political negotiations with British leaders whom he regarded as his equal, work with people from different castes, religions and nationalities to achieve harmony in co-existence, fight for his country's independence and set the highest standards for his people. All his work for civil rights, India's independence and active propagation of love and peace wouldn't have been possible if not for his firm conviction that all people possess the innate capability to change from within, in the pursuit of what's right.

What did I learn from this story? That the person you see in the mirror everyday is the person responsible for your life. You can unlock your innate potential yourself. Who would have imagined that the shy and introverted boy who refused to stay back after school to interact with his classmates for fear of being laughed at, would eventually be able to speak with such eloquence and persuasion, that he could win over an entire nation in his pursuit for India's independence? Who would have expected that the young timid lawyer who ran away from a courtroom would be able to stand up against tyranny and injustice?

It would be easy to say that Gandhi had the good fortune to meet a good mentor who was able to see the potential in him that others didn't. But the truth was, there was no such person in his life at that time. But Gandhi didn't wait. He took accountability for himself. His enlightenment started from the realisation that no matter how his environment changed, if his mentality, attitude and internal mettle were still the same, he would never be able to break through his circumstances. And when he stopped blaming others, the piece of filth clogging his visibility removed itself, allowing him to see the crux of his problem. Himself.

Ellesse Chow

Another Chance

We were vacationing in Goa and, as was our routine, we went to the beach in the morning. I decided to go into the water, while my family stayed back on the beach. I was standing in no more than knee-deep water when, in a flash, a strong undercurrent swept me away.

By the time I got back my breath I found myself deep into the sea, far away from the coast—the people standing on the shore appeared just a few inches tall. I tentatively tried to feel for ground but there was nothing. The horror of my situation struck me completely at that moment.

My first instinct was to scream, and I started shouting for help. After wasting a few precious breaths I realised it was useless, for no one could hear me. I didn't see how anyone would be able to help me either: I was too far out for anyone to swim up to me, and there were no boats around.

I began swimming towards the shore, but each stroke forward seemed to take me further back into the sea. The currents were very strong, and my muscle power was no match for the mighty ocean.

The images of my wife and son flooded me. What misery and shock they would go through. I could almost see my dead body being carried towards them. Tears swelled in my eyes and dissolved at once in the sea. Would it take away my life that easily as well?

The thought of family gave me a spurt of energy and once again I started my Herculean task towards the shore. I swam for what seemed twenty-five minutes, but did not find myself any nearer the shore. Exhaustion overcame me and I let my body go slack; I was giving up. Even today I remember the gulp of salty sea water which tasted of death as I started sinking.

It was then that I had this image. I am a great believer in Hanuman ji and I remember seeing his distinct form, commanding me to swim diagonally. All this time I had been swimming in a straight line towards the shore. Ten minutes of swimming diagonally and the people on the shore became a little larger. I knew I was making progress. About fifteen more minutes and my feet touched the ground. 'Life!' was the word that echoed in my mind.

My son and wife ran up and hugged me as I reached the shore. An entire paramedic team was there as well; the doctor examined my lungs and declared me absolutely fine.

Today when I think back and question the reason why I am still alive, how I had the strength to swim for fifty minutes, I come to these answers: I learned later that my wife Vandana, who works with under-privileged and destitute women, called the ashram where a few of them stay. In no time the word got around and within minutes the ashram was full of children and women praying for my safety. She called my family members and each member—even distantly related cousins—had prayed for me. She called my factory workers. They all stopped work and prayed for me. I guess God *had* to listen to their prayers. If it had not been for the instruction 'swim diagonally', I am sure I would not be here writing this piece.

And of course the love of my family, which gave me the mental tenacity to keep on when giving up seemed so tempting.

This happened four years back and I am a changed man. Now I do not lose my temper as I used to. I go beyond myself and help the needy (and not think that my wife is doing enough for the both of us), and I try to spread happiness as much as I can, for I know now that there is a very thin line which separates life and death.

Ashok Agarwal

God Moves in a Mysterious Way

The insightful poem *God Moves in a Mysterious Way* by William Cowper had fascinated me right from my childhood. I recently happened to reflect on it with a new perspective.

These days, I play with a Rubik's Cube frequently (I have learned to solve all six faces of the cube—thanks to notes on the internet). Our son loves to watch me play, especially liking to see what he calls 'cubies' of the same colour gathered on a side of the cube. Sometimes I solve one face just to entertain him. When I start, he is happy to see red 'cubies' gathering on a side one by one. But as I move closer to solving it totally I have to temporarily 'break' already gathered cubies for the larger goal of solving the whole side. And, since he does not know the underlying logic of this, he gets upset that I am spoiling the side.

It occurred to me once, when this had happened, that this is perhaps exactly what happens with us when we do not see things going our way. Perhaps God is temporarily 'spoiling' our plan so our prayer can ultimately be fulfilled!

I have experienced one such mysterious move while I was a student. My parents had hoped that I would become an engineer, and I had planned to do so as well, but these dreams were shattered when I did not do very well in my Std. XII exams, a crucial element when getting admission into an engineering college.

It was while I was doing the MCA course that I had ultimately opted for, that I realised the grand plans of the Almighty. I realised that I loved what I was doing—engineering was something my parents had wanted me to do, and I was sure that I would not have enjoyed it as much as I did the computer applications course that I was doing. However, it took three more years for my parents to appreciate this shift in plan. After I graduated, I was offered a well-paying job—a job that was offering much more than what they had expected. This, along with the fact that I loved my work, convinced them of what William Cowper rightly said:

The bud may have a bitter taste,
But sweet will be the flower.

God *does* move in a mysterious way!

Harsh Thakkar

Lessons from an Oyster

There once was an oyster
Whose story I tell,
Who found that some sand
Had got into his shell.

It was only a grain,
but it gave him great pain.
For oysters have feelings
Although they're so plain.

Now, did he berate
the harsh workings of fate
That had brought him
To such a deplorable state?

Did he curse at the government,
Cry for election,
And claim that the sea should
Have given him protection?

'No,' he said to himself
As he lay on a shell,

Since I cannot remove it,
I shall try to improve it.

Now the years have rolled around,
As the years always do,
And he came to his ultimate
Destiny stew.

And the small grain of sand
That had bothered him so
Was a beautiful pearl
All richly aglow.

Now the tale has a moral,
for isn't it grand
What an oyster can do
With a morsel of sand?

What couldn't we do
If we'd only begin
With some of the things
That get under our skin.

Author Unknown

Lessons of Failure

Lord, are you trying to tell me something?
For...

Failure does not mean I'm a failure;
It means I have not yet succeeded.

Failure does not mean I have accomplished nothing;
It means I have learned something.

Failure does not mean I have been a fool;
It means I had enough faith to experiment.

Failure does not mean I am disgraced;
It means I dared to try.

Failure does not mean I don't have it;
It means I have something to do in a different way.

Failure does not mean I am inferior;
It means I am not perfect.

Failure does not mean I have wasted my life;
It means I have a chance to start over.

Failure does not mean that I should give up;
It means I should try harder.

Failure does not mean that I will never make it;
It means that I need more practice.

Failure does not mean that you have abandoned me;
It means that you must have a better idea.

Source Unknown

The Boy who Wanted to Fly

Abdul craned his neck to see the Indian Air Force helicopters thundering past with the Indian Tricolour. His eyes misted over when he recalled his passion to fly ....

It was the day of reckoning. He had been waiting for this day—right from the day he had first made aeroplanes from discarded sheets of paper. The graceful flight paths the planes traced before nose-diving to the ground had kept him occupied for hours together. Experiments with various papers, making planes of different sizes and varying wing spans used to go on for hours before Abdul realised that he had forgotten to eat.

Abdul was an ordinary boy with an extraordinary passion— a passion to fly. There was nothing odd about that. But coming from a small town, and just six years old—it was unusual. However, Abdul's father had not found anything wrong with his ambition. The soft-spoken boy was good in studies, in fact excellent; he was religious, obedient and extremely well mannered. There was really no harm in pursuing a hobby, his father reasoned.

Meanwhile, Abdul devoured all the books in his school library that were even remotely linked to flying machines. He sat for hours poring over books, gazing at old black and white pictures of fighter planes until he had committed them to memory. He noted down machinery specifications, engine power ratings, propeller rpms, mach speeds, anything and everything aeronautical he could find. The passion had soon taken over his life and assumed feverish proportions until that fateful day—the day of reckoning.

Abdul had applied for the Indian Air Force. The call for the interview arrived in a simple brown envelope with a Government of India seal. A simple white sheet indicated the date, time and venue for Abdul to present himself to the selection board. That day had arrived. Abdul repeated a simple prayer, over and over in his mind and plunged headlong into the entire test routine.

The mental aptitude test was easy, at least the Math and Science papers. The paper for testing his language proficiency skills was not easy, but it wasn't difficult either. It came as no surprise when the selection board president, a Wing Commander, read out his name in the preliminary screening list.

The next round was tougher. It was a routine designed to test the physical endurance and strength of the candidates. Abdul, despite his frail frame, put his heart and soul into the tasks. He ran around obstacles, jumped over fences, crawled under barbed wires, climbed ropes and shimmied down them unmindful of scuffed knees, chafed palms and tortured lungs. Honest sweat shone on his brow at the end of twelve minutes of exertion. He knew that he had given it his best shot.

Abdul's hopes rose when they were put through the next stage—a medical examination where an Army Major put him through stringent inspections of his heart, lungs, eyes, ears, feet, knees and spine. At the end of it all, the candidates were herded into a hall, where they were told to wait. The results would be announced soon, the Sergeant had said.

Two hours later—when Abdul was feeling faint, not having

eaten since that morning, the Wing Commander walked in with a clip-pad in his right hand. Feelings of nausea were pushed to the background, as Abdul's stomach knotted in anticipation. The Wing Commander read out from his record of short-listed candidates—twelve names. Abdul was not one of them.

It was only the prayer that his father had taught him that made Abdul stand upright that day, even in the face of rejection. It was only the prayer that comforted Abdul when he threw his face down onto the pillow that night. It was only the prayer that roused Abdul from his dreamless sleep and sent him bristling with new found hope to deal with the challenges of another day.

Abdul craned his neck to see the Indian Air Force helicopters thundering past with the Indian Tricolour. His eyes misted over when he recalled his passion to fly. That was a long time ago. The rejection had almost demoralised him, but he had moved on. That was indeed a long time ago.

He took his seat as contingents of soldiers in starched uniforms went by marching in step, saluting as they passed him. It was a special day for the President of India His Excellency Hon'ble Dr A.P.J. Abdul Kalam. He was presiding over the Republic Day celebrations at Rajpath, his heart filled with patriotic fervour that had only grown stronger with time.

As for his passion … the boy who wanted to fly did fly: in a Sukhoi-30 MKI in an official capacity and as the Supreme Commander of the Armed Forces.

Vinith Aerat

Beautiful in My Eyes

I was eighteen when I left home to attend college in New Delhi. I had done well in my Board examinations and easily secured admission to one of the most prestigious girls' colleges in the city. I made new friends, loved my course and was literally on top of the world. About four months later, I went to bed one night feeling unusually tired. Over the next couple of weeks, I'd often feel exhausted in the middle of the day. I put it down to a busy daily schedule, rigorous coursework and irregular meals, till one day when I fainted in class.

I was rushed to hospital and was placed, heavily sedated, in the Intensive Care Unit. When I woke up, I saw my parents and older sister; they had come down from my hometown. Immediately I started to apologise for giving them such a scare but my mother stopped me. She looked at me straight and said, 'Sweetheart, both your kidneys are heavily damaged. We need to find a donor immediately. But don't worry, we'll get through this.' I looked around—my father was sobbing unashamedly and my sister looked like she was in shock.

From that moment, things changed completely for me. I was shifted from Delhi to Hyderabad to Chennai while my family tirelessly hunted for a donor match. I was poked, prodded and had to go through constant dialysis. As the weeks turned into months, hopes of finding a donor with all the attendant legal hassles seemed remote.

Through that entire time, I found peace only by slowly making myself accept what had happened. I forbade my mother from crying and told my sister that she didn't have to be wracked with guilt because it was me, not her, lying in the hospital bed with tubes poking out from everywhere. Finally, I started praying. I would pray for at least two-three hours every day, begging God to release me and my family from this terrible bondage.

God answered my prayers exactly a year and two months after my nineteenth birthday. The jubilant doctors had found a match! It has been three years since my transplant. I have gone back to my hometown since my health needs to be monitored constantly. The heavy medication has led me to look swollen, my skin has turned blackish-brown and I have unnatural amounts of facial and body hair which I can't remove since I have to be careful of infections. The fear of infection also means that I have to wear a mask covering my nose and mouth when I go out. I have started attending a local college, though a lot of people who don't know about my condition look at me as if I am an oddball. But I continue to laugh and play with my ten-month-old niece. And every time I look in the mirror, I see a beautiful young girl. For me, being alive itself is a miracle and no amount of surface blemishes can take away how beautiful and blessed I feel to still be amidst my family.

As told to Priyanka Chowdhury

6

ON LIVING YOUR DREAM

If you have built castles in the air, your work need not be lost; that is where they should be. Now put the foundations under them.

Henry David Thoreau

Continuum

Whatever you can do, or believe you can, begin it.
Boldness has genius, power and magic in it.

Johann Wolfgang von Goethe

Kamna Chandra knew what she wanted to do when she was about nine. From very early on she had been fascinated with the art of story telling and writing. She told herself that, some day, she would write stories that would be made into Hindi films. All through school and college, she worked towards this goal. She devoured books authored by Jayshankar Prasad, Raghuveer Chandra and Premchand with a passion. She began contributing write-ups for her school magazine, and later for her college manual. She graduated with creative writing as her main subject too.

After her wedding she had to shift to Delhi with her engineer husband Navin, leaving the hub of Indian cinema far back in Mumbai. However, she continued to stay in touch with her goal. Her home inundated with books, Kamna used whatever time she had to her disposal to polish her writing skills. She read, wrote, read some more and wrote some more.

It was during this time that she began freelancing for All India Radio and received great acknowledgement for her work. The administration asked her to take up a permanent job with them, but, a mother of three by then, she decided to focus on her family. She declined the offer, and her free time, even if it was as short as fifteen minutes a day, went into either reading or writing. Soon enough she started sending her short stories to magazines like *Sarita* and *Sarika*.

A few years later, her husband got a posting in Mumbai and so she found herself a stone's throw away from the glamorous, dazzling world of Hindi cinema and movie directors. By then all her three children were well settled in their full-day school schedules. Kamna turned her entire focus on creating a story that could be made into a film.

The first story she penned down was what was to later become the critically acclaimed *Prem Rog*, directed by the legendary Raj Kapoor. But she had to fight her way in. Kamna had written the beautiful love story between a widow and a man from a lower caste with immense passion, and the one director she believed would do justice to this story was Raj Kapoor. But she had no access to him, neither did anyone she knew.

She looked up his number in the directory, called up R.K. Studios and spoke to a person named Harish Bibra. After introducing herself and the purpose for which she had called, she asked for an appointment with Mr Raj Kapoor. Harish Bibra told her to narrate the story to Raj Kapoor's assistant, who would then forward it to Raj Kapoor if he thought it had any worth. Kamna's reply was curt: she said no; she had faith in her work and she wanted her story to be judged by none other then the great story-teller Raj Kapoor himself. She didn't want to take the chance of the assistant being unable to convey to him the beauty of the story.

Struck by her audacity and confidence, she was given an appointment with Raj Kapoor. The two met and India saw

Prem Rog, a sensitive and daring love story. Kamna went on to write other hits like *Chandni*, *1942: A Love Story* and *Kareeb*, the only difference being that now directors approached her, and not vice versa.

All along, Kamna kept her action on a continuum. She kept the ink flowing at one level or another and never lost sight of the writer within (though she waited for almost fifteen years, because of her own priorities), or went into a passive state of not-writing. One thing led to another, she moved from school magazines to college manuals, from AIR to *Sarita* and *Sarika*. Today she writes stories for top banners in Hindi cinema. 'I knew I would reach where I wanted to, for I always supported my goals with my actions,' she says.

Raksha Bharadia

Dreams Do Come True

I was radio jockeying, organising events and dabbling in public relations, and theatre simultaneously, but still felt like something was missing. I couldn't pinpoint exactly what it was though. One day, while preparing to anchor a film-based show, I was trying to find some information on the Telugu film industry and found myself wishing for a magazine on the South Indian film industry in English. At that point it struck me: since there was no magazine of the kind, why not launch one myself? Voila! I got the missing piece in my life. But as soon as the initial euphoria of the idea waned, its practical implications started clouding my mind.

Yes, I had dabbled in occasional writing for my shows, but apart from this, I had neither writing nor editing skills. Besides, I had no clue how I would manage the finances as well as the marketing, since I had no experience on that front. For some reason, however, instead of viewing these limitations as daunting, to me they seemed only challenges that I knew I would overcome. I braced myself to start the magazine and promised myself it would be at par with any other magazine published, be it in quality or content.

I started with writing the concept note on what the magazine would be about. At that time I did not know I was actually working on a business plan, though that was exactly what I was doing. I quit everything I was into at that point of time, and even refused a few tempting job offers which came my way, though I needed them. I knew that the task I had undertaken would require my full concentration as well as time.

Once I had developed the basic idea for the magazine, I started approaching individual people as well as institutions for financial backing. It was then that I understood that to get a loan of the size I wanted, I had to be either economically well-off myself or come from a backward area. I fit into neither category. At times, the fact that I was a woman put off managers from even considering my proposal!

About six months passed and nothing was working out on the financial front; I started losing hope. Since I had quit all my jobs, I was surviving on my savings which were fast dwindling too. A couple of my friends tried to dissuade me from pursuing the project; some called me a fool chasing an impossible dream.

What made me persevere? I don't know, but I do remember enjoying every bit of the work that I put in. I was confident that the magazine would be a success, because nothing of its kind existed. Also, the thought that I must give this project my all or I would regret it my entire life kept me going. The saying, 'On your deathbed, you regret things that you did not do, rather than what you did', gave me courage and emotional sustenance.

I did feel trapped though. Since I had already initiated the process of registering the company, there were government matters to handle which involved money, but my loan applications were rejected one after the other. Several times I came very close to getting funding, but at the last moment it would fizzle out for various reasons— once even religion! It was during this time that I actually realised who my friends were; I lost some, and made stronger bonds with others.

I remember one day when I had a very important meeting. I was really low on cash so I sold my entire book collection. With the money I got, I paid for my taxi fare and other documents which I had to furnish at the meeting.

It was at this point that my family and friends, realising my determination and belief in my idea, came forward to help me, not just emotionally this time, but financially too. My youngest sister broke her fixed deposit of ten thousand rupees and handed the money to me. Small bits came from many quarters as I saw my loved ones share their rainy-day savings to help this headstrong girl realise her crazy dream!

Did I feel guilty about using the money? No, for I knew I would make a success of my magazine and money would pour in eventually. I knew I would be able to return their money along with interest.

Finally, nine months later, I launched my magazine *South Movie Scenes*.

The feeling of joy on seeing a product that you have created is amazing! The launch was held at the Press Club and I did not have a celebrity for the occasion. I told myself that I would invite the senior-most person present at the launch to do the honours. I had just about lit the lamp, when I saw the famous yesteryears actress Leelavathi climb up the stairs. I invited her to launch my magazine; she did the honours, blessed me and left. Later I learnt that she was at the Press Club for some television serial and had just climbed up the stairs to use the restroom which was around the corner! I still like to believe that she was there to bless me and to launch my magazine.

Today our magazine *South Movie Scenes* has a readership of about 2,50,000 and we are going international in 2008!

I hear youngsters saying that, some day, when they have enough money, enough time or enough courage, they would like to do something or try something that they have dreamed of doing. I want to tell them that the day they decide to follow their dreams is the right day and the right time. Just believe in yourselves and, yes, it all begins with a dream.

Prathibha

It's Never Too Late

No matter what one says of the status of women in our society, it's almost always difficult for a woman to follow her heart. This is the quest of that woman who dared to make a difference to her life when most tend to give up and accept their fate with an uneasy resilience. Compliment Farhana Khatri, today forty-five, on anything and it will be gracefully passed on to Allah. However, you can also sense the satisfaction she feels for what she has accomplished. She may be better off today, but she hasn't let the memories of those bad times fade away.

'I still remember those days, sitting at home in the afternoons, with nothing to do in that silence. Even a crow on the window would disturb me. I did nothing but pray all day and expect God to listen to me. After all, if the Almighty listens to everyone, why wouldn't he listen to me as well?' she asks. Family problems and personal dissatisfaction combined, and the tension took a toll on her body as well, the signs of which were evident everyday. She suffered from thyroid and even occasional fits. The decision to change her life came when she was thirty-eight. She decided to go back to college. Though a good student, Farhana had to stop studying when she was married off at an early age. 'I knew I had to do something with my life. I decided to pursue a course in journalism. Apart from the usual objections, what made it more difficult was the poor financial condition of the family. In such a situation, a thirty-eight-year-old woman spending money on education was seen as useless,' explains Farhana. However, she knew that this was perhaps the only way she could break out of her situation. She decided to sell her jewellery so she would have enough to pay for her course. 'I still remember that day, when I sold my gold. I came out of the store with that money and just stood there for a while, wondering whether I had done the right thing,' she says. And then, when she started her course, 'A lot of flak came in from relatives and others as well. "What is this woman up to at this age?" they would remark. I used to come home at nine after college, and staying out till nine in the evening was a big deal.'

However, that one decision turned her life around. It was almost like she was re-born in a world that offered her almost anything she wanted. It was difficult though. 'Every small thing was a struggle, especially the projects. The kids today are so techno savvy, using the Internet etc., of which I knew nothing. I used to buy books from the roadside for my research, write out all my projects, with cut outs of pictures. I submitted fat journals while other kids gave slick printouts.' But there was so much to learn. 'The more I went to college,' she says, 'the more I realised how petty things were in the four corners of my home.'

Time would justify her hard work. 'Memory was a big problem. I realised that, at that age, I simply couldn't memorise even a single paragraph. However, by God's grace, I stood first in class. My children were very happy when they saw their mom enter home with a trophy in her hand,' laughs Farhana.

Before she graduated she found a job. She didn't know how to operate a computer at that point, but soon mastered it. When her husband passed away, her relatives expected her to sit at home for the traditional four-and-a-half months. 'You can't expect the breadwinner of the family to do that, can you? Even Islam would support me. On the eleventh day after my husband's death, I was back at my desk,' she remembers proudly.

Today, working as a special correspondent and page editor for a newspaper, Farhana has come a long way. She says she never complains about her workload. 'When I see small children selling newspapers at traffic signals trying to make a living with every penny they earn, what should we complain about? Till the time you have work and are able to work, you have no right to complain whatsoever.'

Farhana believes that a person's happiness lies within herself. 'Nobody other than you can provide for your happiness. It has to come from within. Someone can be your companion to share things in life, happy and sad, but you can't hold him responsible for what you don't have in your life,' she says.

Life is a jigsaw puzzle of emotions and everyone has their own share of times when they feel they're walking a tightrope. It's important to discover oneself as an individual; that is when the dimensions of life change forever. And it doesn't matter if you think you are late; after all, it's never too late to change. As Frederick E. Perl puts it, 'I am not in this world to live up to your expectations, and you are not in this world to live up to mine. You are you, and I am I, and if by chance we find each other, it's beautiful.'

Vikas Hotwani

Self Worth

At one of my classes with a group of adolescent slum children, I asked them to make a chart under the heading 'I am great and I do great things'. The chart would be divided into two parts: the first was to deal with the great things they were doing at present, and the second the great things they would do in the future. Most of the children in the group had dropped out from school after Class 7, mainly for economic reasons, and were currently working as domestic staff.

At the end of the class, each one presented beautiful charts, relating the greatness around them. Each one also had a wonderful and touching aspiration for his or her future.

When it was Heena's turn, she walked up to the head of the class and looked at me shyly. She was a tall, slim girl, always wearing a smile which showed her white but badly aligned teeth, and trying to hide her long legs in an undersized frock.

'Yes Heena, show us your chart,' I said encouragingly.

She unrolled her chart and read out its contents in a timorous voice.

In the first column, she had mentioned she was working as a maid at two houses where she swept and cleaned. In the second column, she had written just one sentence: 'I want to become Kalpana Chawla.'

The children had begun sniggering with the first part, and with the second they started laughing. I was stunned, not at the children's response, but at Heena's simple honesty and her sense of self-worth.

Perhaps it was the tears running down my cheeks that brought pin-drop silence to the class.

Then I asked them two questions.

One, how would they like to stay in a house which had not been cleaned for a day or two or a week? How would they like it, if their street, their neighbourhood, their school was not cleaned but instead kept dirty for a week? Was cleaning your surroundings not a beautiful service to be doing? Did that someone deserve to be ridiculed or rewarded?

Second, did they respect the Father of the Nation, Mahatma Gandhi? Were they aware that he cleaned his own house, his porch, and the community toilet?

Then I asked Heena to repeat what her ambition was thrice. With each time her voice became stronger, more confident.

No one sniggered or laughed. When Heena finished, the whole class applauded.

That day, on my way home, a realisation of my responsibilities struck me ... I had to lay the foundation for these dreams, to ensure that they would no longer just be castles in the air, but reality.

Janki Vasant

Becoming Regina Spektor

New York, I found, was a hard place to make friends and an easy place to write stories. It was summer of 2000 and I had recently graduated from university and had moved from England to New York in order to make my way in the world. I had only the vague dream of becoming a writer and I sent my resumes to publishing houses, believing that was where writers incubated. I was full of confidence and idealistic notions, and devoid of practical ideas. Yet, I was in New York City, posting resumes and typing stories into my laptop.

The city was hot and unfriendly. After the cool evenings and warm friendships of Oxford, where I had gone to college, the vast, dusty city seemed confusingly alien, and I struggled to make sense of it. After the camaraderie of Kolkata where I had grown up, living by myself in a strange city was a lonely business, and I wrote to stave off the silence.

Then one day I made a friend. I was reading at a bookshop when a girl stumbled over my books and fell onto the floor. We exchanged apologies and one thing led to another and she invited me to a concert. 'My cousin's a singer. She's performing tonight. Why don't you come to the show we'll get a couple of drinks?'

I had no other plans, and eagerly accepted. We took the subway to a tiny bar in the heart of Manhattan's East Village, and she led me to a room where a stage had been set up. A scattered group of middle-aged couples made up the audience and my new friend introduced me to her various relatives who were all there for the performance. Together, waited for the music. And what music it was! A girl with a head of unruly curls sang enthusiastically on the small stage. She had written the lyrics herself, and her young voice rang cacophonously and echoed on the walls. Despite the discordant music, something about her brave, lithe body and eager, raucous singing rent my heart.

'Isn't she great?' an uncle whispered to me, and unwilling to be truthful, I nodded. 'Yes, she's very spirited,' I said and slowly made my way out of my chair and inched towards the exit. As I left, I chanced to glance back at the singer. The girl stood very straight in the dark bar, eyes closed, singing her heart out. Her lovely, youthful face was full of hope and joy and she clutched the mike tightly in her fingers. Despite myself, I stayed until the end and joined in the applause as she finished her song. On a whim, I wrote my email address on the feedback book.

Life settled after that for me. I found a job in Manhattan and made a small group of friends with whom I grew close. I continued to write and soon I had a linked set of stories set in Kolkata. Then life heaved again—this time the recession and a job loss took me to the San Francisco Bay Area where I resolved to wait out the economic downturn. In my spare time, I started to write a novel. The chapters grew slowly, as I grew unhappy with my situation. 'What am I doing with my life?' I asked myself frequently. 'When will I ever be productive?' The lack of challenging work proved to be an abiding burr under my skin and my writing felt less like a dream and more like a toy that was keeping me from reaching real adulthood. In frustration, I gave up writing.

'I need to do more grown up things,' I told myself. 'This dabbling with fiction is keeping me from real life. It's time I grew up and became like everyone else.'

Years passed, I met and married a wonderful, supportive man. The economy improved and I found intelligent, challenging work. Raises and promotions came my way, as did the stresses and worries that accompany jobs. Ever so often, I received a mass email from the young singer in New York—she seemed to be getting on very well. One email gave the details of her show in New York. A few months later I read that she was singing in England, and after several months she emailed ecstatically about her nationwide tour with The Strokes. 'Tried pinching myself, didn't wake up ... so happy!' she wrote. Each time I received a message from her, I dusted off my forsaken manuscript, and reread a few chapters.

Life wore on. Work challenges took up my day and my social life took up my nights. Seven years passed this way. I did not write a single sentence of my novel. Increasingly, I grew exhausted with stress and turned to exercise to help relieve my tension. Every day, I walked home from work, trusting the uphill slopes of San Francisco to flatten my belly and ease my mind. Ever so often, I'd glance at the posters that lined the walls of Market Street, advertising iPods, exciting events or emerging bands. Usually my glances were absentminded, I was always too engrossed to truly pay attention. Until the day I saw her—my youthful friend, the singer at the dingy bar. It was unmistakably her—the wayward hair now trendily coifed; that wide, joyous smile. She was going to be singing in The Independent, arguably the best concert hall in SF. Her face grinned at me out of scores of identical posters, her happy face mocking my cowardly, adult life—my inability to commit to my dream, my hesitation to take the risk of finding happiness through my art.

I stood before that poster for what seemed like an eternity, looking at the vibrant face of Regina Spektor, who had once been just a young girl, singing her heart out in a dim, nameless bar. When I got home, exhausted in a way that had nothing to do with exercise, I looked for her on Google. Her music was everywhere: she'd sung tracks on Grey's Anatomy—a show I followed avidly—and her fan following worshipped her music. Tentatively I downloaded a song from iTunes. If somewhere in my envious heart I was hoping for that youthful voice I had heard so many years ago, then I was sorely disappointed. Regina Spektor retained her old throaty notes— but how everything else had changed! I listened mesmerised as my laptop belted out song after song, each more melodious and moving than the other. Her voice was trained and controlled yet fresh, eager, sincere. As she sang, I saw again that face, that hopeful, joyous voice. That courage.

It took me some time to make the change. Time to save money and gather my thoughts and dust off my laptop. Time to read through and discard my old manuscript and to quit my job, and become a full time writer.

This was eight months ago and I wish I could say that this story has had a happy ending. But truthfully, it's too soon to tell. But I have published a handful of well-received stories and have completed the first draft of my novel. I don't know whether my literary adventure will serve as a cautionary tale, or whether it will be a celebratory story of success. But that day, standing at the crossroads of my city, I knew I would never forgive myself if I did not try to live my dream. If I did not give my art my best effort and risk my stable, everyday life to achieve something I consider meaningful. I knew that day that I would never forgive myself if I did not at least try to be Regina Spektor, who had always known how to raise her hopeful voice and sing from her heart.

Pia Chatterjee

I Believe

Miracles happen. Angels exist. But to experience them, you have to believe.

Twenty two years before, when I began my journey, the response had not been flattering.

'Why do you want to be a dancer? That's not a man's profession! If you want to be creative, why don't you get into advertising or something?'

'No one will marry the girls who come to your dance class. It's just not respectable!'

'Why are you teaching those vulgar Western dances? Is India falling short of artistic expression? This is not our culture!'

People sniggered behind my back and criticism rained down on me every day that I danced and sang. But I plodded on, holding that magic umbrella called Faith. But the path was not easy.

I was always in doubt, always insecure; I was always pushed against the wall. As a child, I was too old to play with the children in my housing society and too young to hang out with my brother's friends. I never enjoyed my school life. I was painfully aware that I was different from others, and I felt like a misfit.

As a young man, I fell in love madly with a wonderful girl who eventually was unfaithful to me with my best friend, and I was completely broken. I felt I had no direction. Back in the '70s, there was not much by way of theatre in Bombay. There was one ballet school, and you would see one musical every three or four years.

So I was very hurt when people laughed at my dreams of being a performer. Then I thought, maybe my dreams were foolish. I felt like a victim because I was stupid enough not to trust myself. I never thought my kind of dance would work in India. Back then I didn't even want to dance. My first passion was singing.

One day, as I flipped through a magazine, I came across the photograph of a woman named Khorshed Bhavnagri, and a story about her. I read that her sons, who had died in a car crash, now communicated with her from the afterlife, guiding those who came to her for help. As I read the words printed there, they struck a chord of recognition in my heart. But I didn't want to write to her. I said to her photograph—give me a sign, something that only I will understand.

Sometime later, my friend Zareer Lalkaka called and asked me to come over. When I was at his house, I noticed some people in the hall, and I was impatient for them to leave so that Zareer and I could talk. When I went over to meet them, one of them turned out to be Khorshed Bhavnagri.

I was completely shocked, but also tremendously inspired by the way Khorshed Aunty came into my life. After I met her and read *The Laws of the Spirit World,* my life changed. She taught me how to be giving, how not to hurt myself and others, how to turn negativity into positivism. I have always believed that there is life beyond death, that there is great power in positive thinking. What Khorshed Aunty did was confirm it for me, because I am only human, and I too had many doubts. She told me to start dance class, and I cried, 'Oh God! I don't want to be a dance teacher!' She just smile and asked, 'Why not?'

Being a teacher taught me that you still learn from your students. Being a teacher, you become the eternal student. I learnt from my experience with the Bhavnagris that help is always available to those who ask. But you have to be careful what you ask for, because you may focus and visualise very hard on your goal, but what you ask for may not be good for you, or you may not be ready for it.

When you believe in yourself, you learn to be honest, and live the prayer or the good intention, to embody it. Reading books and praying is of no use if you don't go out in the world and do what's right.

Inner peace is a constant struggle because every day there's change, and every day you have to find you peace. Your spirit is like a wild animal, your mind has a thousand thoughts travelling here and there. One has to learn to control the mind and be a master of it. What I have learnt is that all of us are equal, but we're not the same. And you cannot depend on anyone else for you happiness. Don't blame the world for your trouble, start closer to home—change yourself.

Shiamak Davar

7

ECLECTIC WISDOM

Life is like a game of cards. The hand you are dealt is determinism; the way you play it is free will.

Jawaharlal Nehru

A Painting on the Wall

Often things happen in your life and you are so busy dealing with them that you miss the almost imperceptible changes that have occurred in your own existence.

There is a painting that has sat silently on the walls of the several homes I have known over the last almost half a century. The painting is nondescript. It is actually a messy patch of colours daubed on a piece of canvas by a five-year-old and corrected by the master strokes of a young painter. This unique piece of art is signed and dated. Today that young struggling artist is a very famous exponent of Indian art. A few days back my daughter stormed in asking whether I had got the painting valued. I remained silent. The last few years have been one of intense struggle in our personal lives and much of what was taken for granted has been taken away from us; but somehow, till this moment, I did not realise how different my life had become. I guess that acceptance and surrender had slipped in my life as a gift from God. It is also strange that the big picture theory that was always propounded by my father whenever something hurt terribly and that had been forgotten in the times of plenty, was often quoted by me to assuage every one depending on me for answers.

What had happened to change the once-easily disappointed person into one that accepted life without condition and resistance I do not know. Perhaps it is the fact that seven years back I left my egocentric existence and decided to give back some of what I had received. Maybe it is because the problems that needed to be addressed did not concern me but someone else. I cannot say. I can only share that as my personal resource dwindled to nothing, every time funds were needed to reach out to the children of Project Why they appeared from nowhere, and I saw my once abysmally lonely existence filled with human beings from the world over.

My daughter's question about the value of the painting came back to my mind. How did one value that painting? Easy some would say: browse the net, get an appraiser and so on. But let me tell you the story that lies hidden in every stroke of that painting. The painting was the result of a little girl's weekly trip to a studio, ostensibly to learn painting. However, the little girl carried with her a huge tiffin carrier filled with food that she had been told to 'forget' and leave back at the studio each time. That forgotten food ensured that the young artist did not go hungry for many days, without feeling humiliated. This was probably one of the first lessons my parents crafted painstakingly for me, part of a big picture, one I would understand much later.

So how does one value a painting that holds in it the very essence of what I was to become? This is a question I have no answer to. I hope I can find some way of bequeathing this to my children, but here again maybe there is another part of picture I do not see and the painting will land one day in an auctioneer's hall for some very valid reason.

Yes the big picture exists, one just has to open that part of us that has the ability to see it and then life becomes wondrous.

Anouradha Bakshi

A Reason to Smile

My friend and neighbour Sujata was the average, God-fearing, conscientious housewife, whose life revolved around her home, husband and children. Our lives moved along parallel paths; our children were of similar ages, both our husbands worked in the textile trade, we both fasted on Tuesdays, and went regularly to the temple. The only difference was our luck in household help! Mine came and went with irritating regularity, whereas Sujata's old-timer Anandibai had been with her for years! I envied the relationship between the two: Anandibai cared for Sujata's home and children like her own and Sujata ensured that Anandi's son Ram was fed, clothed and educated. When Ram made it to the SSC merit list, Sujata made the laddoos with her own hands!

Our paths diverged when Sujata's family migrated to the US. I met her again after a gap of fifteen years, in a clinic in Houston. She had cancer, and I dreaded visiting her and seeing her pain. Yet I had to.

I walked in expecting to see a shadow of her former self, but was delighted to find her cheerful and smiling. I hugged her and told her she looked great. 'The bald and the beautiful,' she quipped, referring to her obvious hair loss. I marvelled at her courage in the face of such adversity and was telling her as much when her doctor walked in.

'Well here is the reason for my faith and courage,' said Sujata, signalling towards the young man. 'He loves me too much to let me go!'

The doctor smiled at Sujata. 'You are partying again!' he joked, and turned his gaze to me. Before I knew it, he had crossed the room and was touching my feet.

Sujata laughed gaily, seeing my utter confusion. She finally decided to dispel my confusion, 'I am pleased to introduce you to the brightest oncologist in Houston, Texas, Dr Ram Chitale!'

I felt goosebumps as I embraced the young doctor. Anandibai's son had come a long way.

Sujata certainly had reason to smile!

Vinita S.

Before Life Passed Me By

I distinctly remember the years between 1993 and 1997. They consisted of days when I was leading the exciting life of a film star. I was acting in films, moving around with the biggies, finding myself being quoted in print articles and interviews, getting attention from desirable women, leading an enviable existence. I began to believe that everything revolved around me, that I had it all. There were periods when deep down I felt empty, that life was meaningless. And although I was surrounded by people all the time, I often felt alone. And lonely. I did have my friends around me, cheering me up, and making me smile. I began to believe the feeling of importance they gave me. Slowly, I began realising people need one another, often only to enhance their own sense of success. I began to wonder if I was a success myself, just having some hits to my credit apart from constant attention.

Realisations dawned on me . . . slowly, yet surely. The lifestyle we lead, the car we drive, the cell phone we use and the holidays we take, define and equate our success. I was trapped by a feeling of emptiness. I was only living a life of motion, there was no fun or happiness in my life. The chase for success or glamour is an idle exercise in futility. Slowly, no director, no woman, made me feel good. Or even happy. That is when I met Rajlaxmi, my wife now. She stabilised my wandering spirit. She had implicit faith in God. 'Do your best and leave the rest to God' is what she religiously practiced and strongly believed in. She got lots of books, spiritual ones. And I had never read any of those; I was only into novels. Slowly, I began doing puja, and that is what made me feel humble and calmer. It was not chanting the mantra that made an impact but feeling it, understanding it and imbibing it that made all the difference. The soul of every spiritual or religious book teaches us the essence of what is good, how to be soft, gentle and happy in disposition. I began to know and feel that the mantra of happiness is the same as it was a thousand years ago. It's the idea of success that is distorted in people's minds. Thereon, I quietly began adopting a sense of spirituality. I tried to learn and gauge just how much was enough. Children today want cars and cell phones at a very young age, and in the rush to provide them with these things, parents often forget to ask them to enjoy what they already have. The Bhagavad Gita and the Vedas have changed my life. They have taught me to love, but be free of attachments. Every time I read these books, a new perspective comes to me. My belief in the self has gotten stronger. If I am in the right, nothing in the world should have me back out. I have learnt that. And believed it too.

Rahul Roy

The Five Thousand Dirhams

I am a single mother and run a small business in Dubai. In 1998 I was in a financial crunch. I had just put both my boys in one of the best private schools in Victoria, Canada. School fees were steep and I landed back in Dubai with very little spare cash in hand. I knew that I would need to work day and night to manage things from thereon.

When I landed in Dubai I found my driver Chandra Bhaan waiting for me at the airport, in tears. His father had passed away and he had to fly down to India immediately. Between sobs he requested for an advance on his salary to take care of the extra expense for the funeral ceremony. The little I had would go towards his tickets; how on earth would I be able to find the extra money he needed so desperately? I felt deeply that it was my responsibility to help my staff in their time of need; I had to find a way out for him. I told Chandra Bhaan that I would put him on the first flight to India and wire the money before the ceremony. I had no clue how I would manage to put together the sum, but if I refused to compromise on my children's education, how could I refuse Chandra Bhaan an amount that I knew he genuinely needed. I believe strongly in God and knew that something would come up.

About two days after he had left, I received a letter from one of my banks in Dubai. It was not a bank I used often, and I had been intending to close my account there for a long time. I knew I had a balance of about fifty dirhams in the account, but the account statement they sent showed a credit of five thousand dirhams! It was the exact amount that my driver had asked me for! I knew it was not my money, but the timing of the letter, along with the fact that it was the exact amount that I so desperately wanted for Chandra Bhaan, made me feel that Providence had a hand in the situation. I decided to accept the loan of five thousand dirhams and promised myself to return the money to the bank as soon as my economic situation allowed me to. At that time, Chandra Bhaan's need seemed supreme. I went to the bank that very day, withdrew the amount, closed the account and wired the money to Chandra Bhaan.

Business eventually picked up and I slowly put away dirhams every month to repay the bank. About six months later, I got a call from the bank requesting me to meet the manager. I met the manager who informed me apologetically that they had made a mistake: one of the employees had deposited someone else's money in my account. He told me that if I did not repay the amount, it would be cut from the employee's pay cheque. I immediately pulled out my cheque book, wrote out a cheque for five thousand dirhams and handed it to the manager.

The employee responsible for the mistake, who had been standing there, thanked me profusely; he said he sustained a family of five back home in India on his one salary. 'Actually, I should thank you for the loan,' I said.

I truly believe that when you want something in life and you believe in yourself, all forces of the universe work to help you achieve that desire—with or without your knowledge.

Sonal Rawal

In Faith

It was the year 2002. After many months and late nights behind a computer in a cyber café at Bangalore, I had gained admission to do my Masters in New Media at the London School of Economics. Now, all that remained was getting my student visa to the UK. But, for an Indian student applying to do their post-graduation in the UK, this is everything. After all, it's not uncommon to get rejected at this last stage, even after clearing all your previous hurdles successfully.

I scored particularly badly on the finances front: I had not been able to win a scholarship and I was a self-funded student. A combination of a student loan and my personal savings would cover my stay in the UK, but there remained a deficit that I hoped to cover with a part-time job in the UK. All of this contributed to giving me all the markings of a potential illegal immigrant to the UK.

Worse still, I had decided not to lie or produce any fake certificates to make me look better. I was going to do the right thing and take my chances.

In those days, if you lived in Bangalore, you had to travel to Chennai for a visa interview. So, I took a day's leave from work and caught the night train to Chennai. I landed in the station in the early hours of the morning. I used the restroom at the railway station to freshen up and change and then headed for the visa office.

It was just six in the morning, but the queue in front of the UK embassy already extended outside the huge compound onto the road. The UK embassy had not seen crowds of these proportions since the time of its inception.

As morning became afternoon and then early evening, I was not making much headway. The situation was made worse by people who arrived later in the day, but still wedged their way to the front of the queue.

It was the law of the jungle and when the embassy closed for the day, I still hadn't got my turn.

I went to check in at a hotel and freshen up. I also called work to ask for an extension of my leave. Then I returned to the queue, which would be forming in the night for the next day.

I returned at 8 pm to find a queue that already extended to the main road. Someone in the crowd was issuing coupon numbers to ensure that latecomers did not gatecrash the queue.

Since the embassy could not cope with the numbers, the applicants had devised a system of their own. The idea was to maintain a list of people as they came in with their passport numbers. Each person was issued a coupon with their passport number as their password. Every group of twenty numbers had a keeper who had to remember the faces of people in that group.

It was a strange show of unity as the applicants chose to accept this gate-keeping system. I was to be the gatekeeper for numbers one hundred and eighty to two hundred. As latecomers typically try to gatecrash the backend of a queue, what happened here would be critical.

So we sat up through the night, exchanging stories, and waiting our turn. At six, the guards opened the gate and the queue surged forward. The coupon system had been abandoned.

In the ensuing ruckus, the guards were informed about the coupon system that had been put in place the previous night and they decided to implement it. Out came the list, people were called forward by coupon number and verified against their passport number.

Then it fell to the crowd to maintain the system. Numbers one hundred and eighty to two hundred had no real hope of getting in. Still they played their role admirably, repeatedly weeding out gatecrashers.

As the embassy closed for the day, over two hundred people had managed to enter and get their visa processed. This was a record of sorts, achieved simply by each of us maintaining the queue.

As things turned out, practically all of us who had waited through the night got our turn. I saw more than ever before that a group of people who work determinedly towards a common goal can achieve much.

Yes, it had been a life-changing experience. But, there was more to come.

Later within the embassy, I stood in a queue again and eyed the passport officials carefully. I particularly wanted to avoid the lady passport officer. But as these things work out, I was assigned to the very same lady.

As she examined my letter of admission to the London School of Economics, I explained to her why I wanted to do my Master's in the UK and how I would support my education.

After my night-long vigil and a day spent under the sun, I was quite sure that I looked like an escaped convict. But, I persevered.

She listened, asked many questions and then she stamped my documents. For some reason, she had decided to give me a chance.

Later, as I walked back to my hotel, a car stopped behind me. I turned around. It was the lady from the visa office. She rolled down her car window and smiled at me. 'Are you happy now?' she asked.

I knew then that my student visa had been an act of trust and a product of faith. More often than not life does give you a chance. Then, it's about what you make of it.

Christina Daniels

Inner Beauty

I went to a park near by and my mission for the day was to spot beauty—other than the physical—in every other person I saw. Since most walkers there were strangers to me, my task was to identify beauty in that fleeting moment before they walked past me.

In some, I heard their lively chatter and saw their exuberance and they were beautiful. I saw a man who was patiently filling every hole in the ground with flour for ants, and that made him lovely. There was one meditating, and the peace reflected on his face made him beautiful.

I could spot something to appreciate in everyone—except one man. He was about sixty and wore a grim expression. He neither smiled nor looked at anyone. He walked with a visible limp and one could see flickers of the pain he was probably feeling.

What would I find to appreciate in him, I wondered. I passed him in the first round, the second, third round … the fifteenth round. To my amazement, this person, who was obviously finding it difficult to walk, was walking more than anybody else there. And then it struck me—his beauty lay in being able to persevere, against all odds.

Raksha Bharadia

Reach Out and Ask

It was a cold monsoon day in Delhi. Drenched by the rain, trudging down a slippery road on her way to her job as a domestic servant, Maryam felt a sense of terrible despair. After the death of her husband three years previously, she had struggled to bring up her two sons as best as possible.

She had fought to have them enrolled in a good school, so that they would have a chance at better jobs later. She worked in three households, doing the dishes, the cleaning and sweeping, the clothes washing, in order to run her own small home and to pay her children's school fees. So far, they had managed.

But in the last week, everything had changed. The school had hiked the children's fees. Her mother had fallen very ill, and the hospital bills were mounting up—some days, Maryam couldn't even afford the medicines her mother needed so desperately. Her father drowned his sorrows at the local hooch shop. And just this morning, they had been told that the jhuggi they lived in was to be demolished: they would have to move to a place much further, start a new life. It would be more expensive for her to travel to work, and for her children to travel to school. Maryam had promised herself that her children would never have to leave school, never be an 'illiterate' like their mother, but with the bills and expenses mounting up, she was afraid she could no longer afford to send them to school.

'Maryam, thank heavens you've come!' said Mrs Khanna, one of her three employers. 'I have unexpected guests, and there's so much to do.' Tired and worried as she was, Maryam quietly shouldered the extra work. But inside she was wondering how much longer she could do this. If it hadn't been for the children, she would have given up.

As she left work that day and prepared herself for the long, grueling bus ride home, Maryam let herself be overcome by despair. 'I cannot handle this,' she thought. 'I have never asked for help for myself.' Through her despair, she had the most surprising thought: 'Why not ask for help? What harm could it do?'

Confused, her mind in turmoil, Maryam didn't notice that she had got down one stop earlier. She sighed, and took her place patiently among the rows of other people waiting for their buses. Now she would have to wait for half an hour longer.

'Excuse me,' said a voice. 'Aren't you Abu and Hassan's mother?'

Maryam turned. It was one of the teachers at her sons' school. 'Namaste,' she said politely.

The other woman said, 'I've been wanting to meet you. Your sons are doing so well, you must be proud of them. It's a marvel how you manage everything.'

Normally, Maryam would have just said thank you. But something forced the words to her lips, 'It's not easy.' She was surprised at herself; she never discussed her problems.

The teacher looked at her and asked, 'Maryam, is anything wrong?' And Maryam found herself blurting it all out, the money worries, having to move house, the school fees . . . The teacher listened carefully. 'Would you come and see me at the school tomorrow?' was all she said at the end of Maryam's outburst.

The next day, Maryam was slightly ashamed of herself. She didn't know what to expect, but she guessed the teacher might have found a way to waive part of the boys' school fees. She allowed herself to hope so; it wouldn't solve their problems, but anything would help right now.

The teacher was there with the principal of the school. They were both smiling as Maryam walked in.

'Maryam, we have a problem,' said the principal. 'We've been looking for someone to manage the housekeeping for the junior school, and it's hard to find the right person. You seemed so capable that we assumed you were busy with your own work. But now we know the situation; we've seen you work so hard to bring up your own children that we know you'll do a wonderful job. But do you want it?'

In a daze of disbelief, Maryam listened as they explained what she would have to do. The work would be hard, the hours longer, the responsibility greater. But she would have living quarters on the school premises, and the boys' school fees would be much lower. She accepted instantly, her heart leaping with a sudden joy.

'Thank you,' she told the two women, 'for helping me.'

The teacher smiled. 'No, Maryam,' she said, 'thank you for showing me not to believe what's on the outside. If we hadn't met and talked, I would have continued to think that you were managing well. And then we would have missed out on the right person, the perfect person, for our school.'

C.S. Madhu

Ruben and Rupert

Often, my mother goes on nostalgic trips, talking about *those days*. And usually, *those days* are the days she spent at our old house. I do not remember them very well, we moved from there when I was four years old. But my mom has very fond memories of that house ... it was her first home after she married my dad. It was here that she began a new life and took on new responsibilities. Here, she made friends who taught her new ways of life. So naturally she cherishes her memories of that place. She talks about how the women played badminton in the common courtyard, and how they unfailingly made fools of each other every first of April. How she used to watch the schoolgirls ride away on their bicycles and wish she could be one of them. How she would wait for evenings to set in so she could go out with my dad. How they would have colony get-togethers and enjoy themselves. And whenever she talks about those days, she never fails to mention Ruben and Rupert.

Ruben and Rupert were twins. One of them would wear a band in his neck (for medical reasons); that was the only way my mom could tell them apart. They used to be our neighbours at the old place. Back then, they must have been about eight years old. Their mother used to be the quiet type. All that my mom remembers about her is that she would go regularly to church on Sunday mornings. But Ruben and Rupert would come over and chat with my mom pretty often. They would bring their books over and ask my mom to help them with their studies. And my mom has always had a way with kids, they seem to take a liking to her instantly. Then when I was born, they would come over to see me. They would be amazed by the size of my feet and fingers. They would burst into smiles whenever I smiled or sneezed or even twitched a little bit. They would talk to me for hours and assume some of my actions to be my responses. They were very excited the day I turned over and, later, when I started to crawl. It became a daily ritual for them. They would return from school, hurry up with their homework and then come and pay me a visit before going out to play. Along with the other kids in the colony, they had come home for my first birthday, and for the next three after that. My dad would organise games and everyone would have fun.

Then when I began to stand up, they had assumed it was their responsibility to teach me to walk. They would each hold me by one hand and walk me around. Very patiently, they would wait for my dad to get back home in the evening, and ask him to allow them to take me out. They would be disappointed when my dad refused. But their spirit never died . . . and they were glad when I took my first few steps all by myself.

Then when I was four, my parents decided to move to another house. For the next couple of years, my parents kept in touch with all the families at the old place and, of course, with Ruben and Rupert. Life moved on—I grew up, my sister was born, I started to go to school, my mom started working again. With time, some of the contacts remained and some just withered away. Unfortunately, we didn't stay in touch for long with Ruben and Rupert. Later, we heard that they were happily married and settled with kids of their own.

So now my mom is left with memories of them. I do not even have those. I do not remember them. I don't remember those two boys who wished me on my first birthday, who tried to teach me to walk. But their names are stored safely in some corner of my heart. And I am sure if, someday, I meet someone named either Ruben or Rupert, I will promptly ask if they have a twin.

Then, Krishna...

Out of the seven empty plots in the colony, ours was only the third occupied plot. So beyond our apartment, there was only a vast expanse of land with shrubs growing wildly around.

Our apartment was itself a new construction and therefore, not fully occupied. We lived on the second floor, and the only other occupants were an old couple on the west wing. So my mom had all the more reason to miss the old place. But this was not to be for long. A Telugu couple soon decided to make the place their home. Newly married, the couple had been very happy to know that they would have South Indians as neighbours. So the bonding happened very fast. No sooner would Uncle leave for his work in the morning than Auntie would come over to our place. She would talk like she had known us all her life. Innocent and naïve that she was, my mom didn't mind her visits, one reason being, she remembered her neighbours at the old place and how they had smiled at her when she had been newly married. So my mom took it upon herself to teach Auntie useful things ... most of it being passed on from her old neighbours.

My sister and I too took a liking to Auntie.

A year passed and another ... and the couple had their first baby—Krishna. *My sister and I would go over to see him. We would be amazed by the size of his feet and fingers. We would burst into smiles whenever he smiled or sneezed or even twitched a little bit. We would talk to him for hours and assume some of his actions to be his responses. We were excited the day he turned over and then, later, when he started to crawl. It became a daily ritual for us. We would return from school, hurry up with our homework and then pay Krishna a visit before going to play.*

By the time Krishna was a year old, the other apartments on the block had been taken. *So, along with the other kids on the block, we celebrated his first birthday together. Then when he began to stand up, we assumed it our responsibility to teach him to walk. We would each hold him by one hand and walk him around.*

When Krishna was four, his father decided to switch jobs. They decided to move to Secunderabad. For the next couple of years, we stayed in touch. But as time passed, the letters dried up. But we hear from their relatives in our town that Krishna is doing very well.

So, now I have only memories of him. He probably does not even have that. He probably does not remember those who wished him on his first birthday, who tried to teach him to walk. But maybe, his mom, like mine, has carved my name in some corner of his heart.

Relationships come and go. But what stays are the memories of the good things these relationships gave you. And that makes you want to build new relationships, even while you know that some day these will whither away, only to be replaced by others.

Deepa Venkatraghvan

Scientific Research on Kindness

A friend asked, 'Someone mentioned to me that research shows that a certain number of acts of kindness a week "sticks"—creates the positive habit. Do you know anything about this, or similar, research?'

We thought we'd compile some useful resources for my friend and the rest of you . . . .

Altruism: a neural kick from within: What motivates people to perform anonymously acts of kindness? Researchers at the National Institute of Neurological Disorders and Stroke in Bethesda, Maryland, wanted to find exactly that—the neural basis for unselfish acts. So they decided to peek into the brains of nineteen volunteers who were choosing whether to give money to charity, or keep it for themselves. They found that the part of the brain that was active when a person donated happened to be the brain's reward centre—the mesolimbic pathway—responsible for doling out the dopamine-mediated euphoria associated with things like money and food. But there is more to altruism: not only does it feel good, it promotes trust. Donating also engaged the part of the brain that plays a role in the bonding behaviour between mother and child, involving oxytocin, a hormone that increases trust and co-operation.

Wired to be inspired: Most theories in social sciences say that people's actions and feelings are motivated by self-interest. So here's a puzzle: why do we care when a stranger does a good deed for another stranger? Psychologist Jonathan Haidt has been pondering this question for years. Haidt uses the phrase 'elevation' to describe the warm, uplifting feeling that people experience when they see unexpected acts of human goodness, kindness or courage—and the power of this feeling to inspire widespread compassion. Examples of elevation exist across cultures and historical eras. While psychology has traditionally focused its energy on studying the origin and impact of negative moral emotions such as guilt and anger, Haidt's work seeks to look scientifically at the compelling effects of goodness.

Beyond human altruism: Altruism may be far more widespread than had been realised. A new study shows that chimpanzees are capable of helping others without any thought of personal reward, demonstrating that young chimpanzees spontaneously and repeatedly helped humans who appeared to be struggling to reach sticks within the animals' enclosure. Elsewhere in the animal world there are many examples of apparent altruism. Dolphins, for example, will support sick or injured animals, swimming under them for hours at a time and pushing them to the surface so they can breathe. However, such examples feature social animals where the 'altruistic' individuals help their kin, which is relatively easy to explain in terms of ensuring the survival of the genes that both share. It's much harder to explain altruism when unrelated individuals help each other—and hardest of all when it is between species.

Why do good?: Why do people do good? A new scientific study suggests that it's not just for an emotional reward: people may actually act selflessly because they're acutely tuned into the needs and actions of others. For decades, psychologists and neuroscientists have puzzled over the tendency of humans to engage in altruistic acts—defined as acts 'that intentionally benefit another organism, incur no direct personal benefit, and sometimes bear a personal cost.' The bottom line, says Duke University professor Scott Huettel, is that altruism may rely on a basic understanding that others have motivations and actions that may be similar to our own. 'It's not exactly empathy,' he says, 'but something more primitive.'

Altruism and the young: The scientist dropped his clothespin, and a wobbly toddler raced to help, eagerly handing it back. The simple experiment shows the capacity for altruism emerges as early as eighteen months of age. Toddlers' endearing desire to help out actually signals fairly sophisticated brain development, and is a trait of interest to anthropologists trying to tease out the evolutionary roots of altruism and cooperation.

Generosity—a strategy for survival: Helena Cronin, sixty-four, philosopher, social scientist, and co-director of the Centre for Philosophy of Natural and Social Science at the London School of Economics, has a different take on the survival of the fittest: 'Look carefully at nature, and you will find that it doesn't always seem brutish and savage. Animals are strikingly unselfish.' Cronin offers a way of coping with shared adversity, a new school of competitive thinking based on the notion of an unselfish gene. Her ideas are a more challenging line of thought and a more accurate reflection of how the world works than the view popularised by Intel's Andy Grove that 'only the paranoid survive'. Cronin's version of Darwinism instead talks about 'pronoia'—the idea that altruism and generosity create more rewards than their opposites do.

So scientists are in on it. Kindness is good, contagious and well worth our time!

Nipun Mehta

The Bundle

A dark night. A sleeping city. A deserted lane. Low structures, abutting black asphalt. No pavements, nor any streetlights.

The hour is just before midnight. A streak of lightning tears the sky, momentarily lighting up a tiny bundle of rags lying near a closed door. It lies under a concrete slab projecting over the broad doorway. Even as the thunder follows, the bundle jerks in the darkness.

The rain falls in great sheets, creating its own rhythmic symphony—splattering on metal, wood, plastic, concrete and asphalt. A car turns at the junction into the lane and brakes to a halt in front of the building. The ignition is switched off but the headlights remain on, reflecting off the glistening asphalt. The bundle of rags remains in the shadows.

The door on the driver's side opens and a large black umbrella springs out. A man scrambles out under it and rushes round the boot to the other side of the car. He opens the front door and holds the umbrella high above his head. A woman struggles out of the car. With one hand she holds her distended belly and in the other she clutches a small cloth bag.

The man helps her with his free hand round the bonnet to the entrance. Neither notices the bundle of rags as they pass it. Nor do they hear the wails emerging from it in the din of the storm.

He rings the bell. A woman, dressed in a doctor's white smock over her ankle-length nightgown, opens the door.

'Professor Sen! What a storm! Here, Mrs Sen, let me help you. Everything is ready.'

The door shuts behind them. The bundle of rags continues to whimper in the darkness and the falling rain.

Professor Sen paces up and down the narrow passage that leads to the closed door of the delivery room. He wishes he could be with his wife. The room was too small to hold all of them: Mrs Sen, the doctor, an assisting nurse, and him. Mrs Sen suggested he wait outside.

He is worried. Was something wrong? They are both in their mid-forties, married twenty years, and for the first time their seeds have conjoined. The pregnancy had not been an easy one for her. She had been frequently confined to bed. But she wasn't *that* old! Women could conceive till well past fifty, couldn't they? Yes, she *was* beyond her due date. Yes, she *had* complained that evening: of heaviness, and a constant dull pain in her belly. When he had telephoned the doctor she *had* sounded worried. Something must be wrong.

He stops pacing. The car—he should move it away from the entrance. Professor Sen opens the door and the umbrella flares as he steps out.

It is still raining, but with less force. He peers up at the sky from under the umbrella. A uniform pitch-black. He cannot even see the rain-bearing clouds. No moon visible, nor any stars. He gets into the car, reverses it, and moves it away from the entrance. As he is about to switch off the ignition, a flash of lightning makes him look up. Through the rain-dappled windscreen he sees the bundle. The rags seem to be flapping in the wind. He makes sure that all the windows are up and the three other doors locked before getting out of the car. He locks the last door and turns. Another bolt of lightning rents the sky. This time the silvery light lingers an instant longer. His eyes are drawn again to the bundle of rags. Something in the way the bundle moves nags at him. The wind has stilled.

He stands above the heap. Sees nothing beyond a dark shape, but senses the life within.

Professor Sen opens the door. In the yellow light that streams out, he looks down. The umbrella falls from his hand.

He lowers himself on his haunches, picks up the damp bundle of rags, and stands up. He cradles the bundle in the nook of an arm. With the other hand he moves aside a sodden rag. The baby's eyes blink for an instant as a drop of water trickles down from the scant eyebrows.

From within he hears the sound of approaching feet. The doctor appears. Her expression is grim.

'Professor, the baby.... I'm sorry....' Her voice trails off as she sees what he is holding.

'Is my wife okay? What happened?' the professor asks.

'Yes, she is sleeping. I'm sorry, the baby was stillborn.'

The professor looks at her, then gently lifts the bundle of rags and kisses the baby on the forehead. Behind him, it stops raining.

Rajat Poddar

The Singing Rickshaw Driver

Standing by the roadside, waiting for an auto rickshaw, I secretly scope the options for a ride installed with one of those absurdly loud sound systems. I am not sure if it has anything to do with the fact that I loved Hindi films growing up, but nothing compares to a little background music to accompany one's daily life. One day, trying to beat the sporadic sprinkles of monsoon before it grew into a pouring rain, I jumped into the first auto rickshaw that answered my call. I lucked out and landed the best sound system I have ever encountered: a singing auto rickshaw driver!

Almost as soon as I sat down, he forgot about me and lost himself in song. I watched him in the rear view mirror, thinking this was a man who was not a rickshaw driver who sang, but a singer who happened to drive a rickshaw. He was not singing because he could, but because he wanted to share the music that danced in his soul. His eyes met mine, and almost immediately he stopped, returning to a world that involved me sitting in the back of his parrot green vehicle. I asked him to continue. Shyness suddenly masked his face, accentuated by the dimple that lingered on his cheek. He smiled nervously and switched his focus to manoeuvring through the hectic evening traffic, congested with pull carts, scooters, cows, pedestrians and cars. The rain was becoming heavier. I asked him to sing again. He hesitated for a few moments, and then slowly began to hum a melody. Soon enough he was belting out a dhairo, a traditional Gujarati musical form.

Surrendering to his voice, I silently watched the city unfold. Two policemen were beating a street vendor, while yelling at him to move his illegally parked cart. The rickshaw driver sang louder. We passed a slum, the area peppered with old men watching the day unwind, children playing and women catching up with one another. Poverty had no place in the picture. The sun began to descend. And then we arrived at my destination. I requested one last performance and my talented friend delivered.

As I reached into my bag to fish out some extra money as appreciation for the invaluable experience, he said, 'Why don't you give me ten rupees less. You appreciate music and music is my life.' We did a back and forth with the money, but he insisted and I finally relented. That day, long after the rickshaw driver left, I could not stop thinking about him and his music. I could not stop smiling.

Anjali Desai

The Wooden Bowl

A frail old man went to live with his son, daughter-in-law, and their four-year old son. The old man's hands trembled, his eyesight was bad, and his step faltered. Every night the family ate together at the dinner table. But the elderly grandfather's shaky hands and failing sight made eating rather difficult. Peas rolled off his spoon onto the floor. When he grasped his glass, often water spilled on the tablecloth. The son and daughter-in-law became irritated with the mess. 'We must do something about grandfather,' said the son. 'I've had enough of his spilled water, noisy eating, and food on the floor.' So the husband and wife set a small table in a corner of the room. There, the old man was made to eat alone while the rest of the family enjoyed dinner at the table. Since he had broken a dish or two, his food was served in a wooden bowl. Sometimes when the family glanced in his direction, he had a tear in his eye as he ate alone. Still, the only words the couple had for him were sharp admonitions when he dropped a spoon or spilled food. Their four-year-old son watched it all in silence.

One evening before dinner, the father noticed his son playing with wood scraps on the floor. He asked the child sweetly, 'What are you making?' Just as sweetly, the boy responded, 'Oh, I am making a little bowl for you and mama to eat your food for when I grow up.' The four-year-old smiled and went back to work. The words so struck the parents that they were speechless. Then tears started to stream down their cheeks. Though no word was spoken, both knew what must be done. That evening the husband took his father's hand and gently led him back to the family table.

For the remainder of his days he ate every meal with the family. And for some reason, neither husband nor wife seemed to care any longer when a spoon was dropped, water spilled, or the tablecloth soiled.

Children are remarkably perceptive. Their eyes ever observe, their ears ever listen, and their minds ever process the messages they absorb. If they see us patiently provide a happy home atmosphere for family members, they will imitate that attitude for the rest of their lives. The wise parent realises that, every day, building blocks are being laid for the child's future. Let us all be wise builders and role models. Take care of yourself and those you love today, and everyday!

Author Unknown

When Sadness Comes

The wings of sadness will lift you off the ground without warning
What of it? Don't pay for your ticket and you will be returned to
the ground safely.

When sadness comes…

Dragging its dark cloak about its feet
And whispering its unhappiness through
The long corridors of your heart—

What will you do?

Invite it to tell its story
But don't encourage it to repeat it
More than once.

And when you have listened
All the way through with perfect
Attention—

Then let your awareness move
To other things.

It will not do to ignore all the other guests
Crowded at your doorstep.

Green buds pointing hopefully to heaven
On the slender branches of trees that have
Waited out the winter without complaint.

A purple flower twined around a wooden post
On somebody's front lawn a royal announcement
That you ought to acknowledge.

The round perfection of an orange
The moment before it is cut and the
Fragrant stinging mist finds your fingers.

The laugh lines that crease the corners
Of the eyes of someone you love dearly
Who is wondering why you are so suddenly quiet

All these things visit you simultaneously
They depend on your hospitality.

It does not suit you to play favourites.

Invite them all in and do not worry
Inordinately about your
Sadness.

If you let it—

It will find its natural place.

And when the dark cloak falls away
And the whispering in the corridors
Ceases—perhaps—

Wisdom will walk in its wake.

Pavithra Mehta

With Time by Us

A few days ago I was sitting on the lawns of the National Institute of Design in Ahmedabad with my friend, a beautiful full moon as our backdrop. We inhaled the scent of the fresh grass; he sipped hot chai and I tasted my memories. Some were bitter, some sweet, but all interesting.

We talked. About so many things. About growing up, growing old, growing apart. Our trials then were so trivial, centering around the next presentation, the mess food and the monthly allowance. We would often imagine what our future would be like and fantasise about our names in lights. Our goals seemed so clear, childishly so. But, that was then.

I remember one night in particular. It was very like the evening I had just spent with my friend, and yet so different. I was in my second year, full of song and stars. My friend was in the fifth year, just stepping into the world. A lot of questions were being raised, about life, money and self.

I also remember being very sure of myself. Sure that I would join an advertising agency, that I would be married by twenty-seven, that I would be living in the most happening place, wherever that be.

My friend was not sure. Not sure of the future, not sure of life, not sure of the tomorrow. I scoffed, he cautioned. I sang out loud, he whispered unsurely. And I was surprised. Was this the same fellow who, only two years ago, had vowed to take the world by storm? Was this the same fellow who kidded that I take his photograph now, lest I don't get the chance to later?

Today, I look at myself and am set on a thinking train. No, I did not join an advertising agency. I got married as early as twenty, settled in Ahmedabad and today, twelve years later and two children wiser, I can sit on that same lawn and feel a strange sense of calm even though I do not see my name in blazing lights.

And why? The answer is simple. As a disciple once asked Buddha, 'Isn't one minute for wisdom too short?' The Buddha replied: 'No, it is fifty seconds too long.' This one pure line encompasses all. If you have a song in your heart and a smile in your eyes, anywhere is the happening place.

I have good health, good friends, a good mind and most importantly, a wonderful family. Today, when my friend and I exchange notes, and when we talk about where we were, and where we are now, it is with a feeling of accomplishment. In the Now and Today, we have the most important thing in our hands: time. With time, we can make anything happen.

That's what makes life ultimately worth it. Time for all the good things in life.

Kiran Sethi

Yuva Unstoppable

I was looked after by Kamla, a woman who worked for my parents, through my childhood. One day, some years after she had stopped working for my parents and had moved back to her village, I went to visit her. I saw her sitting under a tree, just outside the village. I was about twenty kilograms heavier now and wasn't too sure whether she would recognise me. However, she did so instantly; greeting me she said, 'Now that I have seen you I can die in peace.' 'Why are you talking like this Ba?' I asked her, upset.

Tears clouded her eyes as she narrated her sorry tale. She was eight-two years old and, to her family, defunct and useless. They made her do all the household work, gave her very little food, and constantly abused her verbally. On the spur of the moment I asked her to come home with me. Without asking a single question she got up to follow me to the car. Gently I said, 'Kamlaben, would you not like to fetch your things?' She said, 'There is nothing of mine in that house that I need to go back for.'

I brought her home and we looked after her for about two weeks. She put on some weight, but the colour that came back to her face probably had more to do with the peace that she felt in a non-abusive environment rather than the dal and roti that we served her. Understanding fully well that it was not possible for me to look after her on a permanent basis, I took her to an old people's home close by. She immediately took to the place. I visited her often and, during visits, heard the stories of the other residents. All were similar: at the end of their lives, they had been thrown out of their homes.

I decided to form a small, informal organisation that would extend whatever help possible to these fragile, aging, yet beautiful, silver citizens. I spread the word around. In the first visit to the old people's home we were just two, the second visit had five, the third ten. Within ten days the number swelled to forty and we now called ourselves 'Yuva Unstoppable'. The day the organisation celebrated its first anniversary we registered our 550th member.

Most NGOs need either money or manpower, we contributed the latter. We went to orphanages, old people's homes, slums, and gave love—lots and lots of love. We listened to their stories, cracked jokes with them and played games. We asked them about their lives and shared with them, ours.

There is one incident which has stayed with me in particular. We were working in a slum area where the population was predominantly Muslim. A small boy approached us and asked, 'Sahib, tamme namaz nathi padwana?' (Sir, are you not going to read namaz?) I answered that we were Hindus and so did not read namaz. The boy, probably all of six, was visibly shocked. He asked, 'Shruti di, Kaajal di, Hindu che?' (Are Shruti di and Kaajal di Hindu too?) I smiled and replied in the affirmative. The boy then said, 'My ammi always tells me to be wary of Hindus. I will tell her today that Hindu-Muslim theek hai.' (Hindu-Muslim together are alright.)

Amitabh Shah

Eighty-Three Problems

Once a farmer went to tell the Buddha about his problems. He described his difficulties farming—how either droughts or monsoons complicated his work. He told the Buddha about his wife—how even though he loved her, there were certain things about her he wished to change. Likewise with his children—yes, he loved them, but they weren't turning out quite the way he wanted. When he was finished, he asked how the Buddha could help him with his problems.

The Buddha replied, 'I'm sorry but I can't help you.'

'What do you mean?' railed the farmer. 'You're supposed to be a great teacher!'

The Buddha replied, 'Sir, it's like this. All human beings have eighty-three problems. It's a fact of life. Sure, a few problems will go away now and then, but soon enough others will arise. So we'll always have eighty-three problems.'

The farmer responded indignantly, 'Then what's the good of all your teaching?'

The Buddha said, 'My teaching can't help with the eighty-three problems, but it can help with the eighty-fourth problem.'

'What's that?' asked the farmer.

'The eighty-fourth problem is that we don't *want* to have any problems.'

Although we may not realise it, we all have a deep-seated belief that if we practice long and hard enough, our problems will go away. And beneath that belief lies an even deeper one: that our life should be free from pain.

Although these beliefs are what bring us to spiritual practice, a life free of difficulties is not what that practice is about. Practice is about becoming awake to the truth of who we are. As we practice, our relationship to our problems may, in fact, become less burdened. But as conditioned beings, living in a messy world, we will always have difficulties. We will always have eighty-three problems.

Suryacitta

The Flower Girl

I was standing in a line to buy tickets to perform a special puja inside a temple.

It was a short line, but the man inside was counting the money handed to him with extreme care; what should have taken ten minutes had already consumed twenty. I definitely had ten more to go before I left the line.

She stood at a corner, regarding me closely. I caught glimpses of her studying my clothes, my hair, my face.

I was in a simple cotton sari and blouse, and my feet were bare as I had left my chappals in the car, and I think she was trying to decide whether she should approach me, and whether it would be fruitful.

She was not a beggar. Hanging from her hand was an assortment of necklaces, beads, chains, and nestled in the crook of the arm was a matted tray holding lotus flowers.

Pretty flowers, pink and dewy fresh still, despite the heat of the early evening.

She must have been twelve or a bit more, one can't really tell with such girls. Her hair was oiled and plaited, she wore a long skirt and a loose blouse, and pink plastic chappals on her feet.

I wondered at the smoothness of her skin, and the brightness of her eyes. They had none of the deadpan look that is so common among the poor.

She caught me looking at her, and walked forward.

Hell, I thought, now I've done it.

Buy my flowers, she said, they are fresh and the Goddess loves them.

How much I asked; ten rupees, she said.

I knew they were for five each. My clothes must have impressed her to quote double.

They are for five everywhere else, I countered.

Ten for two, Amma, she said, softly. You won't take only one, will you?

Quick thinking, I told myself. She caught my inward smile and smiled back brightly. Take my flowers she said, handing them out.

And my beads are pretty, you can present them to someone. I was a captive audience, I could not leave the line to escape her. And I knew how persistent these sellers at the temple could be.

If I bought her flowers, she would still follow me till I entered the temple, trying to sell me her beads.

Let me get my tickets, and I will buy the flowers before I go in, I promised.

She shook her head and went back. Then seeing the line still static, wandered off.

She was back when I turned from the window, tickets in hand.

Amma, she said, at my elbow. A spirit of irritation flashed through me. I wanted to be quiet and concentrate on the fact that I was going to get an audience with the Goddess. And a pesky flower seller was the last thing I wanted to lavish my attention on.

I told you I would buy your flowers, I said, if you trouble me again, I will buy them from someone else.

Her eyes dropped, and the way her spirit folded up, I felt I had crushed a flower with my words. She shook her head and returned to stand against the wall, looking into the distance. There was time yet for the doors to open, and a quick trip to the washroom seemed necessary.

I motioned to the girl, she came running up holding the flowers in her hand. The washroom was quite clean she assured me, pointing to where it was.

I started out. Wait Amma, she said. I turned. She looked at my feet. Don't go barefoot there, she said, take these, and she quickly slipped her feet out of her pink plastic chappals and offered them to me.

She was in my thoughts when I prayed inside the temple. I prayed that she would find the means to an education, so she would not remain a flower girl.

Sathya Saran

Multiplying Kindness

Little acts of kindness happen around the world even though we seldom hear about them. A perfect stranger offers help in the most unlikely of events and vanishes from the scene. You may never see the person again, but you will forever be changed by his or her touch. In my life, I have not only received help, but I have also been very fortunate to deliver aid when it was needed.

As a young mother in America fifteen years ago, I was standing on my balcony one morning watching a couple of boys zooming by on their bicycles down the quiet street next to our home. It was a dangerous downhill ride and the two boys seemed a bit reckless with their speeds. Suddenly, I heard a loud crash and saw that one of the boys had collided into a small tree. The other boy, who looked shocked and confused, was trying to help him. My own son was ten months old at that time and needed a watchful eye since he was already crawling. Our apartment those days was on the second floor and my son already knew how to pry open the front door. I looked for my house keys, but couldn't find them. So I quickly secured the door to my house without locking it and ran out to see if I could help.

Upon approaching, I realised that the boy was disoriented, wobbly and trying to stand up. He appeared to be about ten years old and the other boy was about seven. The boy who had fallen was tall and quite heavy for my skinny frame to support. But I managed to help him to his feet and walked him gingerly to the sidewalk, setting him down on the grass. He was holding his head in both hands and that prompted me to take a look at his scalp. His blonde hair could not hide that he was bleeding, although not profusely. He had evidently crashed headfirst onto the hard asphalt while falling from the bicycle. I ran back home to fetch water and a towel with some rubbing alcohol.

Although untrained, I delivered first aid with a good wash, a rub, and a compress. Since the bleeding had not stopped, I had to continue the pressure compress with my wet towel. We did not have a cell phone those days and so I instructed the younger boy to race back to his home uphill and bring his mother. I stood there holding his wound, wondering what to do next. Besides, he was weeping and I did not feel like leaving him alone. It felt like eternity standing there, hoping for another soul to pass on that street. I decided to keep the boy engaged in a little conversation so he would not blackout. He was starting to slur in his speech and his sentences were getting muddled. So I continued to talk to him, all the while holding his head. His eyes were closed and his face had a painful grimace. He must have felt strange, in spite of his own muddled speech, to hear from a lady with a strange accent asking him about his family and school. Indians were rare in that part of the state then. This boy was probably meeting a South Indian for the first time!

By this time, I was starting to worry if my baby was trying to follow me out the front door by working his seasoned toddler fingers with the dexterity of a professional burglar. He was capable of such handiwork and much more. It would have been a nasty fall down two stories if he had succeeded.

Luckily on that day, he was unsuccessful in his relentless attempts to crank open the door.

Fortunately, the younger boy returned with a lady behind him racing barefoot downhill. I presumed it was the mother of one of the two. She took over the pressure compress from me, and then took leave, thanking me profusely.

I returned to my home, hoping that the boy had not suffered any major injuries. We moved out of that neighbourhood soon after, having purchased our own home within the same city.

One day, seven years later, I was shopping in a crowded mall when a handsome, tall, blonde teenager suddenly approached me. He had a smile on his face when he looked at me and said, 'Thank you.'

Perplexed, I glanced around; I did not recognise him and I was unsure at first if he really was talking to me. Then, his sparkling blue eyes gazing directly into my confused brown eyes, he said 'thank you' once again.

'For what?' I asked.

'You helped me seven years ago when I fell off my bicycle,' he answered.

I remembered of course, and I introduced myself foolishly. He did not need my introduction—he already knew me! It turned out that he had actually lifted his head to see my face once and remembered me for the next seven years! Teenagers are not supposed to do that!

I asked him what happened after he left the roadside. Apparently the blow was so bad that he had cracked his skull and needed major intervention to heal. He spent a considerable amount of time in the hospital to recover and had obviously done very well since that day. Surgery and ensuing memory loss had not shrouded his mind. He was a young man now, heading to college. But somehow he had plucked me out of a crowd of several hundred people in the busy mall that day to reaffirm that my little insignificant help seven years ago had meant a lot to him.

He gave me a warm hug and thanked me again. I went home happy and very surprised to know that it did not take a lot to please somebody. Unknowingly, I had given him a gift and forgotten all about it myself. But he returned this gift to me with a heart-warming hug and a confirmation that little things do matter.

Ranjini Sharma

More Chicken Soup?

Share your heart with the rest of the world. If you have a story, poem or article (your own or someone else's) that you feel belongs in a future volume of Chicken Soup for the Indian Soul, please email us at cs.indiansoul@westland-tata.com or send it to:

Westland Books Pvt Ltd.
IInd floor, K Block Commercial Complex (near HDFC Bank)
Birbal Road
Jangpura Extension
New Delhi-110014

We will make sure that you and the author are credited for the contribution. Thank you!

Contributors

Ellaeenah is a teacher and an enhanced living facilitator, whose focus is empowering others through wisdom. Her teaching experience of twenty-five years gives her the opportunity to stay young with teenagers and to impart and imbibe knowledge on a daily basis. Her website is http://www.jadefirelight.com.

Suryacitta is a member of the Western Buddhist Order. He leads courses, retreats and workshops on happiness and meditation around the UK and Europe.

Kamlesh Acharya, an MBA from S.P. Jain Centre of Management, Singapore and Dubai, is currently working with a software firm based out of Pune. Writing is a hobby he developed a few years ago. His work has been published on the NDTV, and Godubai Web sites. He was an editor for the Oracle internal magazine and blogs at http://kamfucious.blogspot.com.

Anasuya Adhikari, a post graduate in development mass communication has worked as sales manager and trainer for the last fifteen years with various international companies dealing in reference materials for school children. She conducts workshops for parents in schools of Gujarat to help them develop reading skills in children. She can be reached at anasuya_adhikari@yahoo.com.

Vinith Aerat blogs under the name Svengali. He is a Naval architect who endeavours to put down life's experiences on paper. He firmly believes that a good story is 'good' when it inspires a reader to become a better person. It is a lofty dream indeed, to make the world a healthier place, but he knows that his contribution counts, as does everyone else's. If his story made a difference, then let him know at aerat_v@hotmail.com that he's on the right path.

Ashok Agarwal, civil engineer and a gold medallist, believes in god and hard work. He can be reached at ashok.vandana@gmail.com. An engineering graduate, he currently manages the family business of construction and flour milling.

Padma Agarwal is an avid reader. Children are her passion. Their queer world fascinates her and is a source of inspiration for her.

Seema Agarwal is the editor of *AMA News*, and the author of *Help Your 'Self'*. She can be reached at agarwal_seema@hotmail.com.

Rehana Ali, a post graduate in Botany, gave up a promising career in cytogenetics to become a school teacher. She heads La Martiniere Girls' College's nature club and has lead innumerable excursions to enable children to explore the vast natural heritage of the country. She is an avid reader and an aspiring writer. She can be reached at ali.rehana@gmail.com.

Anouradha Goburdhun Bakshi was voted Citizen One 2005 by the India Today group and in the same year received the Red and White Silver medal for Social Bravery. With a Masters in French, she has been interpreter to the likes of Indira Gandhi and Jacques Chirac. After a period of introspection and the realisation that many 'why's' needed to be answered, she decided to find some of the answers by setting up Project Why in 1998. Project Why works with disadvantaged children in New Delhi. Anouradha blogs at http://projectwhy.blogspot.com and her Web site is: http://projectwhy.org.

Jane Bhandari was born in Edinburgh. She has lived in India for forty years and is a writer and occasional painter. She co-ordinates 'Loquations', a Mumbai poetry reading group, and has authored two volumes of poetry, *Single Bed*, and *Aquarius*. She has also written two collections of short stories for children, *The Round Square Chapatti* and *The Long Thin Jungle*. A third collection of poems and a novel are in progress. She can be reached at janebhandari@yahoo.co.uk.

Sapna Bhattacharya did her advanced diploma in mass communications from the Xavier Institute of Communications, Mumbai and has freelanced with papers like *Afternoon, Mid Day, The Sunday Observer* and magazines like *Eve's Weekly, Femina* and *Star & Style*. Her career in writing was put on hold as she took up the production of the television serial *Amanat* for Zee TV. At present she is busy running her boutique Omakrisna in Mumbai. She can be reached at sapnabhattacharya@hotmail.com.

Tanuja Chandra, a B.A. in English Literature from St. Xavier's college, Mumbai and a Masters of Fine Arts Degree, in Film Direction and Writing from Temple University, Philadelphia, U.S.A., is a film director and writer. Her film *Hope And A Little Sugar* won the best feature film award in the South Asian International Film Festival in New York in 2006. She has regularly contributed articles, book reviews, opinion pieces to leading newspapers and magazines over the years. Writing is much more then a hobby to her, it's a parallel career and an important platform on which one can voice one's views. She plans to direct and possibly produce in the future, several projects for women, of women and by women.

Pia Chatterjee is a San Francisco-based journalist and writer who is at work on a novel tentatively titled *Unreal City*. In her life as a freelance journalist, Pia likes to explore the human aspect of business and technology in Silicon Valley. She can be reached at piachatterjee@gmail.com.

Atul Chaturvedi is an engineer based in Stockholm in Sweden and is currently working with Infosys. He enjoys travelling and playing the guitar.

Mallika Chopra is the author of two books: *100 Promises To My Baby* and *100 Questions From My Child*. She is the creative force and architect behind www.intentblog.com, a popular Web site featuring articles by thinkers from around the world. She lives in Santa Monica, CA with her daughters, Tara and Leela, and husband, Sumant Mandal.

Ellesse Chow, a self improvement enthusiast, writes on goal setting, success and motivation. Her passion in life is to help people reach their full potential. She can be reached at editor@goal-setting-college.com, and her Web site is http://www.goal-setting-college.com.

Ram Cobain is a name under which Ram Jayaraman writes. He is a creative director in a leading ad agency, where he gets paid to think of ideas while playing heavy metal music. His inspirations are Steinbeck, Poe, Coleridge, Stephen King and Vedic literature. He believes that writing is what one must do to be happy, stay sane and touch God. He can be reached at ram.cobain@gmail.com.

Christina Daniels is a communications professional with a diverse background that brings together exposure to training, new media, e-learning, print journalism, corporate communication, developmental communication and research. She holds a Masters in New Media from the London School of Economics and Political Science. She can be reached at christinadaniels22@yahoo.com.

Shiamak Davar is a renowned performer, entertainment designer and visionary. As founder of one of the largest dance and performing arts movements in the world, his mission is to share the joy and magic of dance and the stage with people everywhere. Shiamak has the ability to wear many caps as an accomplished singer, dancer, choreographer, director and dance educationist, bringing his expertise to thousands across the globe through Shiamak Davar's Institute for the Performing Arts (SDIPA). Shiamak's vast international experience includes entertainment design for the Commonwealth Games in Melbourne (2006) and the World Economic Forum in Davos, Switzerland (2006). To learn more about him and his institute you can visit www.shiamak.com.

Anjali Desai has been involved in various social service projects in Gujarat over the last four years. She is also a managing director and editor of *India Guide*, a travel guide company focused on collecting knowledge about travel and culture in India. She can be reached at anjwashere@gmail.com.

Darshana Doshi is a teacher who went on to become a freelance journalist. She wrote for the *Times of India* and the Mid-Day group for about five years and then became the editor of a film magazine, a humour magazine and a weekly newspaper run by private publishers. She is currently working on several projects involving books, namely a coffee table book, a biography and a collection of short stories.

Baisali Chatterjee Dutt has an MA in French from JNU, New Delhi, which she doesn't quite know what to do with, as she's been and still is quite busy with diaper duty. She has two boys who are not just the centre of her universe, but her entire universe. When she's not busy being nurse, chef, storyteller and teacher to them, she can be seen with her precious computer ... or sleeping, standing up! She can be reached at bchattdutt@gmail.com.

Arun Gandhi is president of the M.K. Gandhi Institute for Nonviolence, University of Rochester, Rochester, NY. He is a grandson of Mahatma Gandhi.

Preyoshi Ganguly is a student of economics at St. Xavier's College, Kolkata. Her affair with quizzing began when, as a twelve-year-old, she chanced upon a quiz book at a used bookstore. She has been writing ever since she learnt how to hold a pen. A chatterbox by default, an alternative rock follower by choice, she is a dreamer by heart. She can be reached at natasa1987@yahoo.co.in.

Pallavi Guptaa is a traveller in all respects—she has travelled to over two dozen countries, hosted a travel show on India and has now embarked on her own spiritual journey within. She is also the author of the book *When the Porridge Overflows*. She can be reached at pallaviguptaa@yahoo.com.

Sanjiv Pravin Haribhakti is a consultant surgical gastroenterologist and laparoscopic surgeon. He was also the hon. assistant professor at V.S. Hospital, Ahmedabad. He enjoys reading and writing. He can be reached at prasann@icenet.net

Vikas Hotwani is an entertainment reporter for a Mumbai-based newspaper. When not writing about the glam and glitz of the movie stars, he likes travelling, day dreaming and spending time with himself. He loves food, music and everything simple. He can be reached at vikas.hotwani@gmail.com.

Abha Iyengar is a writer, poet, cyber artist and amateur photographer. Her work has appeared in print and online in India and abroad. Her writing has been published in several titles in the Chicken Soup series. She has contributed to *Gowanus Books, Insolent Rudder, Arabesques Review, Citizen 32* and other literary journals. She can be reached at abhaiyengar@gmail.com.

Vijay Jadav has just completed his graduation in English at RH Patel College. He teaches various computer programs to students at Manav Sadhna, a non-profit organisation that works for the uplift of the poor.

Bhavna Jasra, a postgraduate and university ranker in microbiology, successfully runs an enterprise called First Impression, and is ready to launch her new capital management company, Seraph. Passionate about her work and family, she believes that time management, love and family support has helped her achieve whatever she has aspired for. She can be reached at gautam@jasras.com.

Anjana Jha has been writing for the last three decades and been published by major newspapers and magazines including *Statesman, Times of India, Hindustan Times, Eve's Weekly, Femina* and *Woman's Era*. Though fiction is her first love, she enjoys writing human interest and travel articles, and profiles. She has also edited a number of books and publications. She is presently based in Mumbai. She can be reached at anjanajha04@yahoo.com.

Sanjeev Kapoor is one of the top chefs in the country. He has authored several books and is the host of *Khana Khazana*, a popular cookery program shown on Zee TV every Sunday since 1993.

Raja Karthikeya loves writing about what he sees and believes in.

He writes prose, poetry and short stories, depending on which chamber of his heart is touched by his environs. He is currently at the School of Foreign Service at Georgetown University in Washington DC. He can be reached at raja.karthikeya@gmail.com.

Hridesh Kedia, an IIT graduate, *is* currently working with the Core Quant Modeling Group at Goldman Sachs, Bangalore. He enjoys trying his hand at games he has never played before, reading physics, and teaching. He plans to join an NGO which works in the area of education. He can be reached at rideshkedia@gmail.com.

Ruqya Khan moved to Dubai, UAE in 1997. She is a freelance writer and has worked successfully with various local and international publications. She has allowed the writer in her to explore all areas of interest—health, beauty, fashion, food, lifestyle, people, parenting and events. It has been a great journey—following the heart to uncover the world of words and growing as a person from within. She can be reached at ruqya.khan@gmail.com.

Anupam Kher is an actor. He was the Chairman of the Censor Board committee and also the Director of National School of Drama between 2001 and 2004. Anupam Kher runs an acting school in Mumbai called 'Actor Prepares'.

Mahesh Killa, entrepreneur and managing partner of Alcan Manufacturing Co., believes that nothing is impossible. He meditates regularly and believes one can achieve anything if one just perseveres. He can be reached at 09331031472.

Pooja Lulla grew up telling fantastic stories about magical people and faraway lands to everyone she met. Now she tells them to publishers, producers and game designers, who make them into books, cartoon series and computer games. She is the author of the best-selling children's book *Angel and a Half* and lives on a hill near the sea in Bandra, Mumbai. She can be contacted via mail at poojalulla@yahoo.com

Lakshmi Madhusoodanan is a mother and an English teacher with a fondness for people, cooking and reading. She has followed the dictum 'why not?' all her life and put her hand to every bit of work that came her way. A teacher at heart, her greatest joy is to see the younger generation growing up and doing better than the previous ones did. She can be reached at lmadhusoodanan@gmail.com.

Shilpa Malhotra, a Delhi-based writer and IT professional, believes that conventions impair imagination. Having experienced the power of words early in life, she has written several verses, newspaper articles, short stories and blogs. Besides her mother, father and husband, her thoughts and writings are constantly inspired by life itself. To connect, mail her at malhotrashilpa@hotmail.com

Nipun Mehta, dissatisfied by Silicon Valley's dot-com greed, went to a homeless shelter with three friends to 'give with absolutely no agendas'. They ended up creating a Web site, and CharityFocus.org— a volunteer-run organisation that leverages technology to inspire greater volunteerism and shift our cultural ethos towards generosity. While Nipun's childhood dream was to either become a tennis pro or a Himalayan yogi, the current mission statement of his life simply reads: 'Bring smiles in the world and stillness in my heart.' Nipun can be reached at nipun@charityfocus.org or through their website: www.charityfocus.org

Pushpa Moorjani is a fund raiser and a coordinator at Swami Brahmanand Pratisthan, Centre for the Mentally Challenged, CBD, Belapur. She freelances for *Beyond Sindh,* a quarterly magazine published from Hong Kong. She has authored three books: *My First Computer Workbook, Learning Computers with Pushididi,* and *Learning Mathematics with Pushididi.* She can be contacted at 09833709277.

N.R. Narayan Murthy is an Indian industrialist, software engineer and one of the seven founders of Infosys Technologies, a global consulting and IT services company. He has been the recipient of numerous awards and honours: in 2000, he was awarded the Padma Shri, a civilian award by the Government of India; he was one of the two people named as Asia's Businessmen of the Year for 2003 by *Fortune* magazine; in 2001, he was named by TIME / CNN as one of the twenty-five, most influential global executives.

Freya Parekh lives in Los Angeles, California where she recently graduated from the University of Southern California's film production programme. She is currently pursuing her directing and producing talents in Hollywood, and intends to move across the world to explore her real passion in the Indian film industry. Her desire is to bring forth the concept of service to others and the community at large through films. She can be reached at freya.parekh@gmail.com.

Jayesh Patel, a young dynamic social worker, is wedded to Gandhian philosophy for all his community-oriented service activities. Having strong faith in the maxim 'if given the opportunity, each one develops', he works for the uplift of slum and street children and the destitute through Manav Sadhna, an organisation he started with his friends Viren and Anar.

Rochelle Potkar writes fiction. In a mouldy drawer, you would find her MBA certificate, incomplete poems, a plan for 2020, old songs, pictures of snow, a murder weapon, an open ticket and very hungry eyes. She can be reached at rochellepotkar@gmail.com.

Rajat Poddar, an avid reader, enjoys history, politics, human nature, human interaction, writing and editing. He is addicted to solitude above else. He can be reached at aaarkp@gmail.com.

Pinakin Purani L. is a B.E. Mechatronics from S.P. University, Anand. He can be contacted at 02717-282082.

Jamuna Rangachari is a writer currently based in New Delhi. Her main interests include positive values, spirituality and holistic living. She has authored two books for children, *One* (a collection of short stories on all the world religions), and *The Magic Liquid*, an adventure tale with a sprinkling of values. She is the assistant editor of *Life Positive,* and her articles have also been published in *Times of India,*

Hindustan Times, Daily News and Analysis, and *New Woman.* She can be reached at jamuna.rangachari@gmail.com.

Sonal Rawal is a single mother living in Dubai for the last twenty-nine years. An entrepreneur she heads two companies, Creations Advertising and Creations Fashion Designing since 1998. She is associated with several charity organisations around the world. She loves adventure sports and has done everything from bungee jumping to kayaking in Victoria, British Columbia. She can be reached at sonalcreations@gmail.com.

Bipasha Roy has a Ph.D. in political sociology and a degree in law from Utkal University, Orissa. She has worked with nautch girls and orphan children in Kolkata for several years. She can be reached at bipasha_roy5@rediffmail.com.

Rahul Roy, thirty-nine years old, has come a long way. From his Bollywood hits in the early '90s to winning Bigg Boss (the Indian version of Celebrity Big Brother), Rahul believes staying calm helps one tread many a path in life. He is, to many, a cool guy, in the real sense of the word.

Sathya Saran is currently the editor of ME, a magazine that goes out with the DNA newspaper every Sunday. Her column 'Me to You' strikes a responding chord in many readers. In the past, Sathya has edited *Femina* which she reinvented in 1993 and tended till 2004, when she decided to explore new pastures. She is the winner of the Bharat Nirman and Mahila Shiromani Awards, as well as the second prize in the Midday Award for the Most Socially Relevant Story, and the Kingfisher Award for Best Fashion Writer.

Prathibha Sastry thinks she is one of the blessed few who has been able to turn her passion into a career. She heads the magazine *South Movie Scenes.* Her interests include coffee, coffee and more coffee, listening to old Hindi songs, reading and watching movies. She can be reached at prathibhasastry@gmail.com.

Tanya Sehgal is a native of New Jersey and a 2006 graduate of Brown University. As a 2006-2007 Indicorps fellow, Tanya piloted library activities as part of a literacy improvement program with Eklavya in Bhopal, Madhya Pradesh. Tanya will continue with Indicorps in a staff capacity and is considering the legal profession. She can be reached at tanyasehgal@gmail.com.

Kiran Sethi is a design graduate from National Institute of Design; she is an educator and is founder director of the Riverside School in Ahmedabad. A mother of two, she enjoys spending time with her children and with the 240 children in the school.

Amitabh Shah is doing his MBA from Yale in non-profit and finance. On graduating, he plans on starting a private equity fund in India that invests in social entrepreneurs. His motto in life is from the film *Rocky* : 'It ain't about how hard you can hit, it's about how hard you can get hit and keep moving forward!' He can be reached at amitabh.shah@yale.edu.

Ranjini Sharma is an engineer by education and instructional designer by profession. She is a resident of Portland, Oregon, USA and lives there with her husband and sixteen-year-old son. Her hobbies are reading, writing and art. She can be reached at on ranjinisharma@gmail.com.

Robin Sukhadia did his Masters in fine arts from the California Institute of the Arts, and has been studying tabla under Pandit Swapan Chaudhuri at CalArts and the Ali Akbar College of Music in San Rafael, California for the past six years. For the past four years, Robin has travelled internationally on behalf of Project Ahimsa, an organisation committed to empowering impoverished youth through music education. He can be contacted at robin@projectahimsa.org.

Harsh Hiralal Thakkar, an MBA from the Indian Institute of Management, Ahmedabad, finds blessings of the Almighty disguised in everyday happenings as an important source of his inspiration. He and his wife Deesha, both Reiki practitioners, are blessed with a son, Param. He can be contacted at harshthakkar@gmail.com.

Vrunda Thakkar, a B.SC/L.LB, believes that life is beautiful. She pursued astrology from Navgujarat College and is an active Tarot reader. She can be reached at vrundathakkar@hotmail.com.

Janki Hiten Vasant is the founder of Samvedana, a movement towards enriching the life of underprivileged children using education as a tool. She can be reached at 30, Asopalav, Thaltej, Ahmedabad 380057 or jankiv@yahoo.com.

Deepa Venkatraghvan, a chartered accountant and a personal finance editor, has a penchant for writing. She would be happy to share her treasure trove of memories with you at deepa.venkatraghvan@gmail.com.

PERMISSIONS

Permissions *(continued from page iv)*

A Miracle Called Commitment. Reprinted by permission of Mahesh Killa. © 2007 Mahesh Killa.

A Very Special Xmas Gift. Reprinted by permission of Anouradha Bakshi. © 2007 Anouradha Bakshi.

Basama. Reprinted by permission of Anjali Desai. © 2007 Anjali Desai.

Our Indian Idol. Reprinted by permission of Jeffery D. Nongrum. © 2007 Jeffery D. Nongrum.

Friends Forever. Reprinted by permission of Vinita Sarin. © 2007 Vinita Sarin.

Hariya. Reprinted by permission of Purani Pinakin L. © 2007 Purani Pinakin L.

How My Life Changed Its Course. Reprinted by permission of Pushpa Moorjani. © 2007 Pushpa Moorjani.

Impervious to Love? Reprinted by permission of Kamlesh Acharya. © 2007 Kamlesh Acharya.

My Magic Carpet. Reprinted by permission of Bhavna Jasra. © 2007 Bhavna Jasra.

No Bananas for My Mommy. Reprinted by permission of Anouradha Bakshi. © 2007 Anouradha Bakshi.

Sharing. Reprinted by permission of Ruqya Khan. © 2007 Ruqya Khan.

Talking of Love. Reprinted by permission of Jane Bhandari. © 2007 Jane Bhandari.

Unspoken Contract. Reprinted by permission of Nipun Mehta. © 2007 Nipun Mehta.

When Tina Met Santa. Reprinted by permission of Pooja Lulla. © 2007 Pooja Lulla.

The Potter and the Clay. Reprinted by permission of Ellaeenah. © 2007 Ellaeenah.